Fourth Down in Dunbar

UNIVERSITY PRESS OF FLORIDA

Florida A&M University, Tallahassee
Florida Atlantic University, Boca Raton
Florida Gulf Coast University, Ft. Myers
Florida International University, Miami
Florida State University, Tallahassee
New College of Florida, Sarasota
University of Central Florida, Orlando
University of Florida, Gainesville
University of North Florida, Jacksonville
University of South Florida, Tampa
University of West Florida, Pensacola

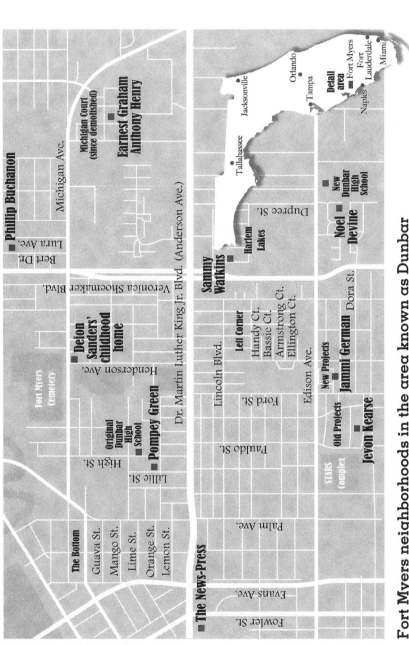

Fort Myers neighborhoods in the area known as Dunbar

FOURTH DOWN
IN DUNBAR

David A. Dorsey

University Press of Florida

Gainesville

Tallahassee

Tampa

Boca Raton

Pensacola

Orlando

Miami

Jacksonville

Ft. Myers

Sarasota

A Florida Quincentennial Book

Library of Congress Control Number: 2014937646
ISBN 978-0-8130-6019-4

The University Press of Florida is the scholarly publishing agency for the State
University System of Florida, comprising Florida A&M University, Florida
Atlantic University, Florida Gulf Coast University, Florida International
University, Florida State University, New College of Florida, University of
Central Florida, University of Florida, University of North Florida, University
of South Florida, and University of West Florida.

University Press of Florida
15 Northwest 15th Street
Gainesville, FL 32611-2079
http://www.upf.com

For my wife

Contents

Driven by Deion

Deion Sanders chewed a Snickers bar as we cruised south on the Dallas North Tollway. The hour-long commute gave him time to think.

Hours removed from an emergency root canal, the numbness and pain had subsided. His mouth seemed to thaw over the course of our ninety-minute interview, after which we piled into his black GMC Savana minivan with tinted windows. It looked like something Mr. T would drive if he, like Sanders, were the father of five.

With his two youngest sons resting in the back, the forty-three-year-old Sanders kept one eye on the road and the other on his phone. I sat in the shotgun seat, keeping one eye on the road and the other on Sanders, who checked a steady stream of text and Twitter messages and fielded business calls via a hands-free headset. Some he answered. Most he ignored. After our interview, he pretty much ignored me, too.

Sanders did not resemble the Prime Time persona he began cultivating in Fort Myers, Florida, where he was born and raised, and where I have spent the last twenty years, after graduating from the University of Kansas.

In 1994, I landed my first full-time job at the *Fort Myers News-Press*. Southwest Florida's first daily newspaper began publishing in 1884. Arriving during the paper's 110th year and at the onset of the Internet and the digital revolution, I had no idea what Fort Myers would end up providing me. I had no clue that I would meet my amazing wife and stepdaughter there or that it would make such a good home for our son, adopted in 2008 from South Korea. When I arrived at age twenty-two, I was recovering from surgery to repair a torn left-knee ligament, and Sanders was on his way to winning his first Super Bowl ring in his only season with the San Francisco 49ers.

My physical therapists warned me not to venture into the place they called Dunbar, especially not after dark. That cautionary remark planted one of the seeds for this book. It sparked my curiosity to find out more about this collection of historically segregated Fort Myers neighborhoods.

Other than a family trip to Disney World, I never had set foot in Florida, and I had not even heard of Fort Myers. I had lived in Saudi Arabia for five years, spent three months in Spain, visited more than a dozen countries, and graduated from the Choate Rosemary Hall boarding school, the alma mater of President John F. Kennedy.

Never in all of my travels had I encountered a place like Dunbar, a dangerous place that also served home to loving, loyal, and vibrant people. They looked after one another, uplifted each other, and encouraged one another to rise from an environment full of poverty and crime. A mystery surrounds Dunbar: Why had so many talented athletes from this small, challenging area reached the NFL? I set out to solve that mystery. Solving it meant getting to know better its most famous former resident.

Sanders began his ascent to fame at Florida State University and then as a professional athlete, first with the New York Yankees and then with three more Major League Baseball organizations and five NFL teams. For fourteen years, Sanders redefined the cornerback position in the NFL, also playing as a return man and wide receiver, winning two Super Bowl rings and making eight All-Pro teams.

But on January 18, 2011, Sanders more resembled a devoted dad than a man eighteen days from election to the Pro Football Hall of

Fame. During the preceding month, I had been trying to arrange the interview with him. I wanted to get his origin story for the *News-Press* to coincide with his sure-fire, first-ballot Hall of Fame election. I called the NFL Network to make an arrangement. No luck. I tried contacting representatives from some of the companies he endorsed. That did not work either. I tried Twitter. At the eleventh hour, he tweeted me back.

"@DavidADorsey: Come to Prosper on Tues. I'll give you all you need and then some. #Truth."

That tweet led to a last-second flight to Dallas and a nerve-racking scene at the iron gate of Sanders's Prosper, Texas, mansion, where there was no answer from him on his phone, his Twitter feed, or the bell at the gate. Meanwhile, my editors were calling me every five minutes, wondering if Deion had backed out of the interview and whether the expensive trip was all for nothing. Deion's wife at the time, Pilar Sanders, finally arrived, to my extreme relief. She explained that Deion had had the root canal that morning and was napping. Two hours later, Deion and I were barreling down the tollway. He allowed me to shadow him for the rest of the evening and the following day.

"Super Bowl week is the play," Sanders told me. "People are on the go before the play. There are a lot of things that have to happen to make sure the play is there."

That first night, I joined Sanders and Shilo and Shedeur, his two youngest sons and members of the Truth youth football teams, on a trip to a Plano barber shop.

Every now and then, Sanders hired the barbers to make a house call in Prosper. Sitting on 100 acres, Sanders's mansion fell just short of thirty-nine thousand square feet. He put the home, appraised at $5.6 million, on the market for $21 million even before 2012, when he filed for divorce from Pilar. The price reflected the uniform number 21 he wore with the Atlanta Falcons, Dallas Cowboys, and Washington Redskins. The estate featured a football field with goalposts outside, an indoor basketball court, a bowling alley, two indoor swimming pools, thirteen bathrooms, three dining rooms, a twelve-acre lake, nine covered parking spots, five fireplaces, and twin spiral staircases leading to the second floor from the base of the front door entryway. A seven-year, $35 million contract with the Cowboys along with the rest of the loot he made as an athlete and pitchman afforded him that home. It also allowed him to get his sons some quality haircuts.

At the barber shop, Sanders took photographs of his sons' haircuts and posted them on his Twitter account. Twitter served Sanders as another avenue to market himself. He began using the online information stream in December 2010. Within a few weeks, he had sent almost four thousand tweets and topped ninety-six thousand followers. By 2014, he had sent more than thirty-five thousand tweets and had more than seven hundred thousand followers.

When the haircuts were finished, we continued to the south side of Dallas and the Oak Cliff Bible Fellowship, a church that had a gymnasium where Shilo and Shedeur had basketball practice.

As Sanders pulled into the parking lot, he saw Ray Elder, an assistant coach for the Truth. Sanders lowered his window.

"We've got to work tomorrow," Sanders said. "We've got to go outside. I want you to put the word out."

A serious look spread across Sanders's face.

"I want 100 percent participation," Sanders said, before raising the window.

"This is all he does," Gregory Upshaw, the father of eleven-year-old Truth player Isaiah Upshaw, told me later. "He dedicates himself to these kids, 100 percent."

Less than twenty-four hours later, Sanders again drove from his home south down the tollway. This time, his children were in school, and he shifted into Prime Time mode following a forty-five-minute workout at his home gym.

Sanders picked me up from my hotel, and we rolled in a different black GMC, a Yukon XL sport utility vehicle. Deion had a business meeting in downtown Dallas with Asim Sheikh, chief executive officer of Zouk, a nightclub. Zouk means celebration in Antillean French Creole.

Sheikh and Sanders were finalizing Super Bowl parties that would be attended by prominent active and retired NFL players and an assortment of models and reality-TV stars. That year's Super Bowl took place at the new Cowboys Stadium.

"It's ladies' night," Sanders said to Sheikh. "And what do you get when you bring in ladies? Men!" Those men would allow Sanders and Sheikh to turn a profit from the party.

On this day, working as a marketing master, Sanders carried himself with the same swagger he showed on the baseball and football fields. Five years after he played his last down, he endorsed GMC, Under Armour, Pepsi, Campbell's Soup, Verizon Wireless, and DirecTV.

Sanders's thirst for attention appeared unquenchable. He stayed connected to the game as an NFL Network analyst. When the cameras weren't rolling, Sanders kept even busier. His vision to unite the best youth athletes in Dallas through sports evolved into educating them as well. When he wasn't filming commercials, he was calling state legislators and securing grant money to start a charter school. He founded Prime Prep Academy in 2012.

All of these endeavors, as well as his desire to be a stand-up father to his five children, stemmed from his upbringing in Dunbar, where the all-black high school closed in 1969 because of court-ordered desegregation.

After the shackles of segregation were removed, the small, impoverished, African-American community in Southwest Florida produced a remarkable crop of nationally renowned athletes. That same community became a violent hub for the illegal drug trade, not just for Florida but for the southeastern United States and beyond. Dunbar introduced America to crack cocaine in its cruelest form. Many in law enforcement circles determined Fort Myers to have been the epicenter of the nation's crack cocaine epidemic of the mid-1980s because of the drug's purity as produced and sold by the dealers there.

The same drug culture that threatened these young athletes, destroying some of the most promising among them, also once protected them, providing teenagers wads of cash, clothes, shoes, and support to keep them out of the drug business and on track toward their goal of reaching the NFL. The code of the streets since has changed. A breakdown in the leadership of the old drug gangs at the turn of the twenty-first century combined with the proliferation of new, more ruthless gang leaders resulted in more competition among them. That competition created more violence, claimed more young lives, and resulted in less protection of children with athletic potential.

Cocaine and the crime that came with it ravaged many Dunbar families, forcing the many extraordinary mothers and fathers, other relatives, coaches and educators, black and white, inside and outside of Dunbar, to protect and salvage their young stars from the streets.

The allure of glory and wealth in sports and in the drug trade deluded so many of the would-be sports stars and drug dealers at a time when life seemed to offer no other dreams for poor, black youths in what remained one of America's most segregated cities.

By the beginning of 2014, Dunbar had produced close to two dozen NFL players. None of them had as high a profile as Sanders, who was inducted into the Pro Football Hall of Fame in August 2011. Yet many became NFL starters, and a few of those became multimillionaires.

As a sportswriter for the *News-Press*, I witnessed these future stars when they played high school football across Lee County. Watching them mature from playing as teenagers to playing on TV has been a highlight of my career. Most of them went on to play at Florida State University, the University of Florida, the University of Miami, or the University of South Florida.

On December 3, 2010, I stood on the sidelines at South Fort Myers High School, where Sammy Watkins IV caught a 69-yard touchdown pass on a fake punt play. He scored again five plays later on a 60-yard punt return in clinching a come-from-behind, 28–21 state playoff victory against Bradenton Southeast. Less than four years later, on May 8, 2014, I stood in Watkins's childhood home. I watched as fifty of his friends and family members piled into his 200-square-foot living room. They watched TV and cheered as the Buffalo Bills made the Clemson University standout wide receiver the No. 4 pick in the NFL Draft. Watkins, who received a four-year contract approaching $20 million, passed Sanders as the highest-drafted player in NFL history who was raised in the Dunbar community.

Dunbar-raised players have, since 1982, played for the Arizona Cardinals, Atlanta Falcons, Buffalo Bills, Cleveland Browns, Baltimore Ravens and Colts, Chicago Bears, Dallas Cowboys, Detroit Lions, Jacksonville Jaguars, New England Patriots, Oakland Raiders, Philadelphia Eagles, St. Louis Rams, Tampa Bay Buccaneers, Tennessee Titans, and Washington Redskins.

Defensive end Jevon Kearse played in three Pro Bowls. Earnest Graham started at fullback. Anthony Henry earned millions as a cornerback and safety. Noel Devine set his county's record for rushing and became a college football star at West Virginia University, only to spend less than a week in Eagles training camp. Jeremy Ware partly achieved his dream, moving from the drug-infested streets of a Dunbar neighborhood called Left Corner to become a seventh-round draft pick by the Raiders in 2010, making the team his rookie year but getting cut thereafter. All of those players grew up without their father in their home. All of those players had family members who were incarcerated for drug-related crimes. All of those players followed Sanders out of Dunbar and to the NFL.

There were others. Some made it big like defensive end Greg Spires, who earned millions as a defensive end for the Patriots and Buccaneers. Others like wide receiver Ed Gant and cornerback Quinton Pointer were on the verge of the big time, toiling on NFL practice squads, hoping to get their big breaks. Pointer caught such a break in 2013, making the fifty-three-man roster for the St. Louis Rams. He entered the 2014 season trying to make the Tampa Bay Buccaneers.

All of the players who followed Sanders hoped to one day attain his moment of football immortality.

When that moment arrived in the summer of 2011, Sanders wore the traditional gold blazer reserved for the fewer than three hundred souls enshrined in the Pro Football Hall of Fame in Canton, Ohio.

Deion Sanders wore an Under Armour lapel pin on the right side of that jacket, a symbol of the money he had made through endorsements. He stood in front of a glass podium at McKinley High School's Fawcett Stadium facing about ten thousand fans and a national television audience.

Sanders revealed the shame he had felt when ridiculed by a North Fort Myers High School football teammate, who made fun of his mother because she cleaned hospital rooms and bathrooms for a living. Sanders's sense of shame became a driving force, launching him on a path to becoming a game-changing cornerback and a multimillionaire with a penchant for pitching products. He became a born-again Christian and one of the greatest athletes of all time.

"He clowned me and he mocked me because of my mama," Sanders said during his twenty-four-minute induction speech, one he began by thanking by name 109 people who had helped him along the way. "So I made a pledge to myself that I don't care what it takes. I'm not going to do anything illegal."

Sanders paused for a second. Doing something illegal would have been easy growing up on the east side of the railroad tracks in Fort Myers. Although moisture formed in his eyes as he reached the climax of his Hall of Fame speech, not a single tear fell.

"My mama," Sanders said, "would never have to work another day of her life.

"When you talked about me, media, guess what, behind you I saw my mama," Sanders said during his speech. "When you wrote about me, when you naysayed me, when you criticized me, I looked right through your TV and saw my mama.

"When you told me what I couldn't do, when you told me what I didn't do, when you told me what I would never be, I saw my mama pushing that cart. When you told me I was too small, I wasn't educated enough, I saw my mama because I made a promise. And whenever I make a promise, there will be a responsibility to that promise. You have to maintain that responsibility. That's why I love this game."

Sanders closed the speech by responding to the critics who claimed he couldn't and wouldn't tackle his opponents.

"I want to respond to that publicly, because that affects me, it bothers me. That's insinuating that I'm soft, and I've got kids. Since 1989, I've tackled every bill my mama has ever given me. Haven't missed one. The next time they say Prime didn't tackle, make sure you let them know: Yes. He. Did."

Sanders focused his speech on the promise he made to his mother and how she inspired him to reach the riches of the NFL. Yet there were forces at work well beyond his mother cleaning toilets at Lee Memorial Hospital in the 1970s and 1980s. There were drugs being sold not far from the corner of Henderson and Michigan Avenues where Sanders grew up. There were father figures in his life, but his biological father and his stepfather each dealt with their own vices of drug and alcohol abuse. There were bills to be paid, and one primary caregiver—Sanders's mother—who paid the bulk of them. Urban influences inspired Sanders to place, at the end of his Hall of Fame speech, a symbol from his upbringing on his Hall of Fame bust: a blue do-rag.

In the mid-1980s, do-rags in Dunbar abounded. So, too, did single-parent homes, low incomes, and crime, a tragic trifecta that exists to this day. Hope for teenage boys came in the form of aspirations to achieve either the neon glitz of Sanders or the fast-filled pockets of the drug dealers.

Dunbar's frenetic pace meant the athletes had to devise ways to avoid trouble. Not all of them did. The carload of young men who shot and killed Washington Redskins safety Sean Taylor during a botched burglary near Miami hailed from Fort Myers. The convicted triggerman is a former high school player and the son of a youth football coach.

Reaching the NFL required playing college football. The college football scholarship trend did not begin until the late 1940s, when "Daddy" Mack Sanders, paternal grandfather of Deion Sanders, patrolled the east side of Fort Myers as its police chief. The trend began in the shade of a corner drugstore off Prince Street and Anderson Avenue. It began with a fellow named Robert Green.

"I have never met Deion," said Green, who in 1955 become the first Dunbar-raised athlete to try out for an NFL team, "but I have always wanted to speak to him. There are a number of people who wonder if I was even faster than he was."

On the corner of Prince and Anderson, at this gathering place of African-American teenagers in 1949, three young men, none of whom Deion Sanders ever has met, unknowingly shaped his destiny. Two decades before Prime Time set foot on Earth, they were pioneers of achieving college football scholarships.

Until 1949, no black athlete from Dunbar ever had received a full college football scholarship. The drug trade, then in its infancy, had yet to take hold of the community. Harry S. Truman served as U.S. president. Color barriers still were being broken by Major League Baseball teams. Segregated Fort Myers suddenly had not one but three high school athletes recruited for college football.

Safety Hill

> There is only one Fort Myers in the United States, and there
> are 90 million people who are going to find out about it.
> Thomas Alva Edison, 1914

The inventor of the light bulb might have been a little bit off in his projection of 90 million people discovering Fort Myers. Thomas Alva Edison was correct, however, in predicting the explosive growth that would hit the City of Palms. By the late 1990s, the population of Southwest Florida approached a half million. Fort Myers serves as the region's anchor and the home of its international airport. Other than for die-hard fans of spring-training baseball, beachgoers, and northerners with second homes there, Fort Myers has remained relatively unknown and hidden south of Tampa and Orlando and west of Fort Lauderdale and Miami. A run to the Sweet 16 by fledgling NCAA Division I basketball program Florida Gulf Coast University in March 2013 also brought the area some positive press. The spring-training home of the Minnesota Twins since 1991 and the Boston Red Sox since 1993, Fort Myers previously served as a baseball winter haven for fans of the Kansas City Royals, Pittsburgh Pirates, Cleveland Indians, and Philadelphia Athletics, who trained at separate times from the 1920s through the 1980s at Terry Park in Fort Myers. New York Yankees legend Babe Ruth once drew the entire town, about five thousand fans, to an exhibition game in 1925 at Terry Park against manager Connie Mack's A's. That manager's great-grandson, Connie Mack IV, eventually became the region's congressman.

Before Fort Myers was established in 1886 with a population of fewer than five hundred, its most famous part-time resident and most prominent snowbird, Thomas Edison, bought property there in 1885. Until his death in 1931, Edison spent his winter months on a Fort Myers estate along the banks of the Caloosahatchee River. Marks of his influence remain throughout the area. A statue of him and his winter neighbors, automobile icon Henry Ford and tire titan Harvey Firestone, sits in the middle of Centennial Park in the Fort Myers River District. Edison's last name adorns the football stadium at Fort Myers High School and a street that cuts through the black community. The intersection of Edison Avenue and Ford Street lies not quite a mile south of the original Dunbar High School. Few whites ventured there, even forty years after integration, unless passing through to the modern Dunbar High School on Edison Avenue or to the former Boston Red Sox spring-training and minor league practice fields.

The original Dunbar High School, built in 1926 on High Street, served Southwest Florida's small pockets of African-American children. Most of them lived in the segregated sections of Fort Myers then known as Safety Hill and an adjacent area nicknamed The Bottom. The school had graduating classes in most years of between five and twenty-five. Robert Green entered this world on May 31, 1928, six decades after the United States abolished slavery and eight decades before the country elected Barack Obama as its first African-American president.

Dunbar High School was named after the esteemed African-American poet Paul Laurence Dunbar, who lived his life like a shooting star. He lived to just thirty-three, a flash even at the turn of the twentieth century, dying in 1906 from tuberculosis. Despite his short life, the son of escaped slaves drew legions of fans. He bridged gaps between worlds white and black, writing some of his poems in conventional English and others in the African-American dialect of his day. Across the United States, not long after Dunbar died, black communities in which he had never set foot began naming buildings and schools and streets after him.

In 1948, when Green and friends Karl Morrison and James Stephens were high school seniors, only the high school and a street on the south side of town had taken on the name Dunbar. Two decades before Dunbar caught on as the black community's nickname and fifteen years before Dr. Martin Luther King Jr.'s "I have a dream" speech, blacks and whites referred to the black neighborhoods as Safety Hill because being there provided blacks security and because the higher elevation prevented flooding in this sea-level city just inland from the Gulf of Mexico.

Televisions, air-conditioning, and electricity had yet to arrive in this segregated community. Blacks were not allowed west or north of the railroad tracks after dark. If they disobeyed, they were hustled back across the tracks to Safety Hill.

Green, Morrison, and Stephens joined a few handfuls of teenagers who gathered at a drugstore in the late 1940s in Dunbar. There could not have been that many there, as their graduating class numbered just eighteen students. One fall evening during their senior year in 1948, Morrison brought with him a photograph he had cut out of the *Pittsburgh Courier*, a reputable African-American newspaper distributed nationally to about 250,000 subscribers. The black-and-white picture showed a grand brick building that stood four stories tall but appeared even taller. It had white columns, white trim, and a white spire. This palace of learning looked like a place of worship. The administration and main classroom building at Allen University, a historically black college in Columbia, South Carolina, grabbed Morrison's attention. So, too, had the affections of his girlfriend. A year older than Morrison, she attended Allen and mailed home favorable reports. There weren't many opportunities for young black men and women from Fort Myers to go to college in those days. Unless their families worked for wealthy whites, they would have little means to that end.

Football scholarships were rare. Only one young black man from Fort Myers had gotten one, and that was a partial scholarship. Roosevelt Grattic, Dunbar class of 1948, went to Bethune-Cookman in Daytona Beach to play football. His parents had more money than those of his peers and could afford to pay the difference. On this steamy fall night, Morrison sat waiting for Green and Stephens. When they arrived, a grinning Morrison showed them his treasured photograph. He suggested the three of them seek college football scholarships together. They spoke not of becoming pioneers, because the idea had yet to dawn on them. They spoke as friends driven to earn a college education.

"We were the first," Morrison said, six decades later. "Like going to the moon. Once we went, it was like when the West opened up, and everyone moved west."

They met with Dunbar football coach Bernard "B. B." Crowder. He followed a one-year stint by Richard Anders as coach of the Tigers. Anders and Crowder were the first two college-educated physical education teachers at Dunbar High School, having gone to Florida A&M University. They realized their students could barter their athletic abilities for free educations.

And, boy, did they have some athletic abilities. Morrison issued Green the nickname "Pompey," which stuck because he possessed the leadership and speed of the ancient Roman military leader. The five-foot, nine-inch, 165-pound Green played halfback on offense and defense. They called the five-foot, eleven-inch, 155-pound Morrison "June Bug" because of his ability to shift speeds. Morrison, who was born on February 6, 1928, played quarterback and defensive halfback. They called Stephens "Big Um," because at six feet, one inch and 185 pounds, he stood out as one of the biggest players of his time. Born on November 3, 1930, Stephens grew into a force as an offensive and defensive end.

Although no one kept statistics in those days, people took note of this: in the 1946 season, when they were sophomores, the three of them led the Tigers to an 8–0 record. They captured an unofficial state championship. Clad in orange and green and wearing hand-me-down equipment from neighboring, white Fort Myers High School, they played all-black schools in Sarasota, Tampa, Fort Lauderdale, and Miami. They did not win as much in 1947 and 1948, but that mattered little.

In the fall of their senior seasons in 1948, Coach Crowder mailed letters to four colleges on the trio's behalf: Howard University in Washington, D.C.; Central College in Durham, North Carolina (which later became North Carolina Central University); Bethune-Cookman; and Allen University. There were no recruiting services or 40-yard dash times or simple ways to scout players. College coaches had to go by word of mouth from their connections in various cities. Or they would look at what was the staple of speed at that time, the 100-yard dash.

As 1948 turned to 1949, letters filtered in to Green, Morrison, and Stephens. All four schools replied. On a perfect, pristine, and paradise-like winter afternoon, the three boys gathered again at the drugstore. They discussed their options.

"Did you boys get a letter today?" Morrison said, pulling his out of a back pocket.

Green and Stephens acknowledged they had. These recruiting letters were the first of what would become thousands mailed to the 33916 zip code.

In the years that followed, the bulk of the letters would be postmarked Gainesville, Tallahassee, or Coral Gables, but in 1949, segregation practices barred Green, Morrison, and Stephens from playing at Florida, Florida State, or Miami. Florida integrated in 1958, Florida State in 1964, and Miami in 1966. The three players knew where they stood. Nothing less than a full scholarship would allow them to become the first in their families to earn a college education.

When Howard University offered them each a five-hundred-dollar scholarship, they were forced to decline. None of them could afford to even catch a bus that far, let alone pay for the rest of the tuition. Central College offered a working scholarship, in which the trio would have to toil in the cafeteria and play football in exchange for the tuition. Bethune-Cookman offered partial scholarships. Finally, they had Allen University, the school Morrison had favored from the start. Founded in 1870, Allen gave newly freed slaves a chance to earn an education. Eighty years after opening, it provided a groundbreaking moment in Fort Myers sports history. Allen offered the three of them full rides on the condition that they make one of the first three teams. In that time, some colleges separated teams into three groups of eleven players. The trio laughed at their good fortune.

"If we couldn't make the first thirty-three, then we had no business playing," said Green, who ran the 100-yard dash in 9.8 seconds upon arriving on campus. Green, Morrison, and Stephens were the first black men from Fort Myers to earn full college football scholarships. They were far from the last. At Allen, Green showcased his world-class speed. He earned an invitation to the Olympic trials in 1952 after running the 100-yard dash in 9.4 seconds.

"I didn't make it out there," Green said of the trials, which were in California. "I didn't have the finances to go. Knowing what I know now, I would have found my way there."

Green then became the first black man from Fort Myers to garner a tryout with an NFL team, signing a preseason contract with the Cleveland Browns, who ended up cutting him because only four roster spots were allocated to African Americans.

Morrison remained a lifelong Browns fan, just because the team once gave his friend a chance. In his eighties, Morrison wore a Browns watch with a leather strap. He recalled how his own family ended up in Fort Myers, which resembled an outpost more than a destination. Morrison's grandfather settled in Fort Myers because the railroad he had helped build ended there. His father also worked for the railroad. His grandmother helped raise him. Morrison's mother died when he was two. Morrison later earned a living as a physical education teacher and coach. After graduating from Allen, he coached in Bluffton, South Carolina, at Michael C. Riley High School followed by stints at Ralph J. Bunche High and Camden County High in Woodbine, Georgia, and Ribault High in Jacksonville, Florida, in a career spanning between 1958 until he retired in 1993. He coached track, basketball, and football. "Coach" became his name. He returned to Fort Myers after retiring and relocated to Jacksonville when his health declined in his mid-eighties.

"You could preach, teach, or go to the farm or be a barber," Morrison said of the job opportunities in Dunbar. "We had three or four grocery stores in the community, and they were owned by whites. They could only hire so many."

Upon arriving at college, Morrison told his new teammates about receiving hand-me-down shoes and equipment. He learned that many of the northern black athletes were better off than ones from the South. "I wore two left shoes, so I didn't even know my right foot from my left foot," Morrison liked to joke.

Green had more time to spend with his mother than Morrison did with his, but not much more. Mary Green died from pneumonia when Robert was nine. Green's father, Isom Green Sr., never remarried. He worked for the head of household of a white family that grew tropical plants and flowers on the other side of the neighborhood known as The Bottom. Isom Green would pick roses and other flowers and distribute them to local churches and funeral homes. In return, he received a modest salary. He never paid a dime for rent.

Robert Green began working at an early age. The youngest of three, he arose each morning at five o'clock. He rode his motorbike to the *Fort Myers News-Press* downtown and retrieved newspapers. He delivered them to the black neighborhoods before school and made twenty-five to thirty-five cents a week. He used that money to buy clothes. For three years, he dropped out of school in order to work, which explains his age of twenty-one at the time of his high school graduation.

Stephens had an even more difficult upbringing and less money than Green and Morrison. Green's father abandoned his family and moved to South Carolina. Stephens's mother, who had given birth to him at a young age, often was in poor health. An aunt and uncle raised Stephens, who, after attending Allen University, returned home and become a basketball coach at Dunbar High School. In 1974 at Fort Myers High School, Stephens became the first black head coach in desegregated Lee County history, guiding the Green Wave's basketball team. Stephens also served as a father figure to the late Isaac Anderson Jr., the first African-American judge in Lee County. Before moving from South Carolina back to his hometown, Stephens crossed paths with an eleven-year-old named Charles F. Bolden Jr. In 1957, Stephens worked briefly as a physical education teacher at W. A. Perry Junior High in Columbia, South Carolina, where he taught Bolden. Bolden grew up to become the head of NASA. Stephens influenced and inspired hundreds of young men and women. He died in 1996. The Lee County School District changed the name of Lee Middle School in Fort Myers to James Stephens Middle Academy in his honor.

"I feel proud for my husband, because he was so poor," said Vera Stephens, who also graduated from Dunbar High in 1949. "In high school, he stayed out a year to work, because his family's house burned down.

He overcame all of those things. He was a grade above me, but with him sitting out a year, we ended up in the same class."

At James Stephens's funeral in 1996, Anderson remembered his mentor.

"In his own way, he wanted all of us to grow up bold and irrepressible," Anderson said. "He wanted to steel us against the inevitable racism we would face and yet not let us forget who we were and what we were about. He wanted us to recognize our true personal worth as individuals who could and would succeed."

Like Morrison and Stephens, Green aspired to coach. After two years teaching and coaching at all-black Smith Brown High in Arcadia, Florida, and at a South Carolina school, Green went on to carve out a thirty-five-year career as an educator, administrator, and friend to thousands as coach and athletic director at Dillard High in Fort Lauderdale, Florida. The Florida High School Athletic Association inducted Green into its Hall of Fame in April 2013. At Morrison's urging, I nominated Green for the award.

"I really go back to my days at Dunbar, and I tell people that during those times we didn't have anything but we had everything," Green said. "We didn't realize that we were poor, because we enjoyed our times, we enjoyed our neighbors, we enjoyed our friends. Let me tell you, we didn't even have electricity. We used a lamp. We had a wood stove. That's how we heated our homes in the wintertime. It was a small community, especially compared to the way it is now. Everybody knew everybody, and we kept our doors unlocked at night.

"I still treasure those days. I was quiet. My actions spoke for me. I was not a big talker. But I will say today that I believe I was the fastest athlete to ever come out of Fort Myers. I believe that."

3 Raising Their Hands

Fast forward more than sixty years and past the turn of the century. Sports agent Drew Rosenhaus stood in front of four hundred children on a hot and humid July morning forty miles east of Dunbar. His T-shirt had his company's Superman-like logo on the front. Instead of an "S," the letters "RSR" were encased within a diamond. The words "Rosenhaus Sports Representatives" were printed in silver lettering below the initials.

The children, ages six to sixteen, sat on a grass football field at the Immokalee Sports Complex, just across the street from Immokalee High School, the center of a low-income, Florida farming community of about twenty thousand residents. The children wore shorts and red T-shirts depicting the white silhouette of a running back, Immokalee's hometown hero Edgerrin James. Several dozen of the four hundred children had taken buses from Miami. An equal number had traveled from Dunbar.

Rosenhaus held their attention.

"How many of you guys are interested in playing in the NFL one day? Let's see a show of hands," Rosenhaus said. He did not offer them any other career options. The children had no problem with that. At least four hundred hands flew up into the air. Some of the children raised both hands. "Well, what we have today are two of the greatest running backs in the history of the National Football League here to teach you some football skills," said Rosenhaus as he motioned behind him to Clinton Portis, of the Washington Redskins, and James, who, just five months earlier, had started as running back for the Arizona Cardinals in Super Bowl XLIII in Tampa.

"Let me start off by introducing Clinton Portis from the University of Miami and the Washington Redskins," Rosenhaus said, and a short round of applause ensued. "He was one of the best running backs in college. Drafted in the first [sic] round. His first two years in the NFL, he played so well that the Washington Redskins said to the Denver Broncos, 'We'll give you Champ Bailey, the best defensive back in the NFL, and a second-round pick for Clinton.' Then the Redskins ripped up his contract and made him at the time the highest-paid running back in NFL history."

Rosenhaus paused for a moment.

"Clinton now makes $10 million a year!"

About thirty camp counselors, mostly Pop Warner and high school coaches from Immokalee, Fort Myers, and Naples, broke into laughter. The children cheered.

"But we all know how much money Clinton makes," Rosenhaus said. "More importantly, he's good to his family. He's a hard worker. He never gets in trouble off the field. You can learn a lot from him. His mom and dad go to every single game he plays. I want a big round of applause for him."

Portis tipped his baseball cap to the children, who clapped for another minute. Rosenhaus continued.

"Next, I want to introduce a local legend. He was one of the best athletes to ever come out of this area. He was super highly recruited out of this area and went to the University of Miami. Fantastic person. Please give a big hand to Jammi German."

German, a 1992 graduate of Fort Myers High School, received first-team and Defensive Player of the Year recognition from USA Today as a senior before moving on to Miami. Five knee surgeries limited his

NFL career with the Atlanta Falcons and Cleveland Browns to four years. German then moved back to his hometown of Fort Myers, taking a job as a security guard at the Alternative Learning Center, a public school for children who had been suspended or expelled from the other public schools. German flashed an ear-to-ear grin and waved to the children. Rosenhaus continued.

"Now, let me tell you about Edgerrin James," Rosenhaus said, as James kneeled behind him. "Not only does he have the chance to be the all-time leading rusher in NFL history, not only has he made as much money as any player can possibly make in his career, but he has been an outstanding person off the field. He's wonderful to his family and to his friends. He has done so much for Immokalee and for everyone here. He's an outstanding role model. But you have to realize that at one point in his life, he was right where you were, right here in Immokalee. Going to school here, growing up in Immokalee. Through hard work and perseverance, he made it to the NFL. Now, he's got five homes. He's got a Lamborghini!"

The camp counselors began to laugh at what sounded like hyperbole. But all of it was true. James had sold his Bentley and purchased, with cash, a pearl-white Lamborghini just a few months earlier. Rosenhaus kept going. He was on a roll.

"He's got everything you could possibly dream of," Rosenhaus said. "But every time I talk to him, you know what he's doing? He is either working out, spending time with his family, or reading a book. I want you guys to learn, not only from his worth ethic and his athletic ability, but that he's a great reader. Instead of playing video games, read a book! As great a player as he is, he's so smart and cares so much about life. He can do anything he wants to. He can play football again. He can retire. He could even own a football team if that's what he wants. So let's give him a big hand!"

James waved to the children and started to rise, but Rosenhaus had one more thing to say.

"I'm going to watch you guys today, because I'm looking for future talent! So I want you to work hard. If you're thirsty, get a drink. You've got the Vitamin Water tent over there. We're going to have a great time.

We're going to learn a lot about football. Most of all, have a lot of fun, guys. Thank you. Have a great day!"

Great days have come in bunches for Rosenhaus and his clients. He has negotiated some of the largest, longest, and most lucrative contracts in NFL history, making himself a multimillionaire in the process.

The Dunbar community has been good to Rosenhaus. When he told the children he was looking for future talent, he was not kidding. Rosenhaus has had four Dunbar-born or -raised athletes as clients: running back Earnest Graham, cornerback Phillip Buchanon, defensive end Jevon Kearse, and offensive tackle Mario Henderson.

James, a free agent at the time of his 2009 summer camp, thereafter signed a one-year, $2 million contract with the Seattle Seahawks. Although James did not grow up in Dunbar, he had plenty of connections to the Fort Myers neighborhood. His former high school principal grew up there, and he lived in a neighborhood with many similarities to the Dunbar community, where many of the children grow up with no fathers, little money, and little hope for a promising future.

Although Rosenhaus painted a pretty picture for the children, the statistics told another tale. Only one in fifty high school football players receives a college scholarship. Of them, 30 percent fail to make it through college and earn a degree.

Only eight out of every ten thousand high school football players—less than 1 percent—get drafted each year by an NFL team. Of those drafted or signed by an NFL team, 78 percent go bankrupt within two years after retiring, according to *USA Today*.

Many Fort Myers teachers and coaches counsel Dunbar teenagers and younger children to develop a "backup plan." They have it all wrong. Plan B should be Plan A, because the odds of reaching the NFL are pretty much the same as the odds of winning a lottery. Plan A means pursuing athletics as the only way out of poverty and hopelessness. Others choose the swift but perilous path to easy money by dealing drugs. Dunbar didn't always used to be that way.

"It's hard for me to say what it is now," said Jeremiah Primus, who graduated from Dunbar High in 1961 and served as Immokalee High School's principal during Edgerrin James's time there as a student.

"When we were growing up as youngsters, our schools were segregated. Dunbar was a typical school that you'd find in the South. You have many times inadequate equipment. When I was growing up, we didn't see things like high pregnancy rates among the girls. We didn't have so many kids doing drugs. You hardly heard of anything like marijuana. It was something kind of foreign.

"In '61 when I graduated, we were still a little sleepy town. I don't even think we had twenty-two thousand people then. It was just Dunbar and the Fort Myers Green Wave. I don't think we had anything else. Here's the difference between then and now. We had somewhat of an understanding that whoever was an adult, you give your respect to that adult. If an adult found you doing something wrong, they would tell you, and you would stop.

"All they had to say was, 'I know your father' or, 'I know your grandfather.' We looked out for each other. We went to our scout meetings. I don't even remember if we locked our doors or not. Everyone seemed to look out for everyone. There was a certain expectation of behavior. We didn't go beyond that. Daddy Sanders, when he told you to get off the street corner, you got off the street corner. He was one of the guys you respected."

As the years passed, many of Dunbar's youths turned to dealing drugs. The ones who fathered children often left them, either leaving town to escape the law or leaving for jail when law enforcement finally caught up to them. Of the good young men from Dunbar who did graduate and move on to college, many never returned home, having found better chances and places of employment in northern cities.

The lack of father figures helped to make Dunbar a troubled and dangerous place.

"You've got kids in middle school now smoking marijuana," said Riley Ware, a 1985 Cypress Lake High School graduate who went on to play football at Western Kentucky University and in the Arena Football League. His son, Jeremy Ware, would grow up to play football at Michigan State University before being drafted by the Oakland Raiders. "It used to be that drugs were for the older guys. Adults were using it. But right now, you're talking about middle school kids using cocaine. You go to middle school now, that's all the kids are talking about, drugs."

There weren't many African-American doctors or lawyers in Fort Myers. Although there were quite a few schoolteachers and school administrators, there were too few role models for Dunbar's youth other than those who had made it out of the neighborhood by playing sports.

And there were plenty of those.

"Deion Sanders, he changed the whole game of football," said longtime Fort Myers resident Frankie Raybon, whose brother Ed Gant played briefly on the Tampa Bay Buccaneers practice squad. "He did. This is the way I look at it."

A college football recruiter once told Raybon, "We come to Florida to find the best football players in the United States. But we come to Fort Myers to find the best defensive backs in the United States."

Dunbar's Dynamics

The racial makeup of Dunbar has changed little in the sixty-plus years since Green, Morrison, and Stephens graduated from Dunbar High School. Many other things have changed. Most black-owned businesses were sold, went bankrupt, closed, or relocated. By the early 1970s, the drugstore where the three college-football-playing pioneers had gathered in the 1940s long since had been flattened into a parking lot. Anderson Avenue, named for the first physician in Fort Myers, became history as well, renamed in 1991 after civil rights activist Dr. Martin Luther King Jr. The boulevard served as one of the primary entrances to Fort Myers from Interstate 75, which prompted city officials to order the widening and beautification of the road. Palm trees and tropical plants were placed between the east- and westbound lanes. The widening forced even more black-owned businesses to relocate or close.

The 33916 zip code encompasses Dunbar. It is bordered to the north by Palm Beach Boulevard and to the south by Colonial Boulevard. To the east lie Marsh and Ortiz Avenues and Interstate 75, and to the west are the railroad tracks, which were laid out by African Americans not long after slavery ended.

In 2010, the *News-Press* profiled that 33916 zip code, reporting the unemployment rate at almost 30 percent, more than double Lee County's 12.7 percent. The area had 20,000 residents. One-third of the adults twenty-five and older, about 4,560 people, did not graduate from high school, more than double the Lee County number. Those who worked did not work for much, with the average income hovering just above $16,000 a year.

By day, men wearing white "wife beater" tank tops rode bikes throughout Dunbar. Laundry hung on clotheslines outside housing projects and apartment complexes. Young men walked in the neighborhoods, some of them with their shorts pulled below their buttocks, with plaid or black boxer shorts hanging out the back, and gold capping their teeth.

On Fridays and Saturdays, the streets appeared deserted between dusk and 2:00 a.m., when hookers and onlookers and teenagers and twenty-somethings spilled out of nearby nightclubs, returned home, or crowded around roadside food stands on the corner of Ford Street and Dr. Martin Luther King Jr. Boulevard.

Welcome to Dunbar, where there are no welcome signs designating it as a named neighborhood. Anyone from Fort Myers can tell you how to get there. Newcomers and vacationers to Southwest Florida, however, would have a tough time finding it without asking a local. Dunbar has no mayor, no chamber of commerce.

The black community's businesses may have been better off in 1969 than in 2009. Other than a sprinkling of convenience stores, barbershops, and hair salons and two gas stations, Dunbar had no center of commerce more than a decade into the new century. There were no major supermarkets, only small, neighborhood corner stores. One of them, Pop's Grocery, generated more than 164 calls for help to the Fort Myers Police Department in 2010. In the preceding fifteen years, there were at least nine shootings at the store, several of them fatal. Residents of Dunbar must leave the neighborhood and head west and over the railroad tracks in order to shop for bulk groceries or even eat at a McDonald's.

Dunbar High School opened in 1926 and moved from High Street in 1963 before closing in 1969, following the court order for desegregation.

A new Dunbar High opened in 2000, and the court order expired in 2003. The court order both developed and damaged the black community.

"Desegregation was the best thing that ever happened to me," said Leon Church, who was born in the 1950s, attended Dunbar High, and then transferred to North Fort Myers High in 1969, graduating from there in 1972. Church, the oldest of nine children, including his brother Calvin Church, a high school All-American linebacker, made friends with white students when finally given the opportunity. Leon Church said he never would have done so without integration. He learned that some white children were raised to believe that blacks had tails between their legs. Walking to downtown Fort Myers as a young child, Leon Church would get off the sidewalk if he passed a white person, following his mother's lead. They drank from water fountains labeled "colored." They had things easy compared to the African Americans in Mrs. Church's native Alabama. Still, "this place was backwards," Leon Church said. "At the time, it seemed normal to me. Looking back, it was awful."

The white community of Fort Myers found an easy and convenient label for all of the formerly segregated neighborhoods: Dunbar. When the black children arrived at the formerly all-white schools for the first time in 1969, the white children called them the "kids from Dunbar," short for Dunbar High School. "Dunbar" came to mean the black section of town. For the blacks who lived in Dunbar, these neighborhoods had their own distinctive personalities. Each was unique, different even from those just a street away.

Levon Simms, who coached Deion Sanders in basketball, taught at North Fort Myers High, and later became a Fort Myers city councilman, took me on a tour of Dunbar several years ago. He taught me about the nuances of the different Dunbar neighborhoods.

Most of the neighborhoods within Dunbar have two-word names. Southward Village, a government-subsidized housing project, built in the 1960s and childhood home of Jevon Kearse. Franklin Park, home to teachers and nurses and coaches. Lincoln Park, a palm tree–lined avenue that in the 1980s and early 1990s showcased drug dealers and buyers, shaming the legacy of the street's namesake, President Lincoln. Johnson Quarters. Hope Gardens. Highland Circle. Harlem Lakes. Palmetto Court. Michigan Court. Aqua Shores. Brook Hill. Cypress Courts. Whitehead Creek. Jones Walker.

As a young child, Deion lived in Jones Walker, an apartment complex. About a mile south sat Left Corner, a series of four dead-end streets that could be reached only via left turns while heading south on Henderson Avenue. The Left Corner streets were named after jazz greats W. C. Handy, Count Basie, Louis Armstrong, and Duke Ellington.

Velasco Village—better known as The Bottom—was located just on the other side of the railroad tracks, the oldest black neighborhood in Fort Myers. It took on the nickname The Bottom because of its location at the bottom of the tracks and because of its lower elevation than the rest of Dunbar, previously known as Safety Hill.

"Fort Myers is unique," said Simms, who for years lived in Franklin Park. "There is only one Fort Myers. No matter where you go, you'll never find another place like it."

Within Dunbar, there's no place like The Bottom, with its five streets named after the fruit trees that used to grow in abundance behind them: Guava, Mango, Lime, Orange, and Lemon Streets run east to west. In that order, they descend, north to south. All of them intersect with Cranford Street, which leads south to Dr. Martin Luther King Jr. Boulevard.

"We called it Dodge City," Larry Gary said of The Bottom. Gary grew up on Guava Street. Like Deion Sanders, Gary played high school football at North Fort Myers High School under Coach Ron Hoover. Gary, a linebacker, grew up to become the first black varsity head football coach in Lee County. Lehigh Senior High School hired Gary when it opened in 1994, exactly one quarter of a century after Lee County schools were integrated. In 2014, he coached the Cape Coral High team.

"Growing up in The Bottom, it was always a little crazy," Gary said.

So far, not one athlete has made it out of The Bottom to become a professional football player, yet the neighborhood influenced all of the athletes from the rest of Dunbar who did. Just as Harlem epitomized and set cultural trends for African Americans in New York City, The Bottom did so for African Americans in Dunbar. One young man did emerge from The Bottom to become a professional athlete. Walt

Wesley, who was mentored by James Stephens before graduating from Dunbar High School, class of 1962, attended the University of Kansas. The six-foot, eleven-inch Wesley then embarked on a ten-year career in the NBA with eight teams, averaging 8.5 points and 5.5 rebounds per game. Wesley returned to Fort Myers after coaching in college. He involved himself with youth athletes while overseeing the Fort Myers Police Athletic League.

"I lived on Mango Street, right by the railroad tracks," Wesley said. "As a kid, I was always watching the trains go by. Across the street was Michigan Park. That was really nice. You had people in the neighborhood selling snow cones. There'd be a guy with a cart on wheels, pushing it around. My mother was from Fort Myers. She was born in 1912 and raised in Fort Myers."

Wesley also knew Daddy Sanders, Deion's grandfather.

"He was a great person," Wesley said. "Everybody loved Daddy Sanders. He always had time for you. Communication was amazing back then. You could be on one side of town, but by the time you got home, if you were doing something bad, the news would beat you home. The information would get back there before you did. And we didn't have cell phones of course, and some people didn't even have telephones."

Wesley lived in Fort Myers in two different eras. He refused to let the lack of equality be an excuse for not achieving a college education. Then again, Wesley had schools courting him as a student because of his skills on the basketball court.

"It was about applying yourself," Wesley said. "Educational opportunities have always been there. You had to work a little harder for it back then, and it wasn't as open as it is today. You didn't have as much accessibility to it. Florida, Florida State, and those schools, they were not recruiting black athletes then. That just wasn't an option at that time."

When Wesley returned to Fort Myers in the early 1990s, he had been gone for almost thirty years.

"It was 180 degrees different," Wesley said. "When I left, we were in segregation. When I came back, it was integrated. That in itself speaks volumes. The county lines and the city lines had extended. Everything had grown. The high school I had gone to was no longer the same school. They built new schools and expanded the schools. Government housing, those things were taking place. Of course, that was happening all over the country. It wasn't indigenous to here."

Rosemary Tape has nothing but fond memories of growing up in The Bottom with her brother Ronnie Tape. The street names were not for nothing. "I'd give anything to go back to that time," she said, her face curved upward into a smile, remembering all of the fresh fruit. She used to make jam from the guava trees behind her house on Guava Street.

"The sights and the smells and the tastes?" Rosemary Tape said. "Nothing could beat growing up in The Bottom."

In the 1950s, The Bottom endured a heroin epidemic. While the older generation grappled with heroin and alcoholism, the younger generation began turning to sports as an escape.

One child born near The Bottom in the late 1950s would go on to become the first man from Dunbar to play in an NFL game, the first man who attracted Division I college football recruiters to Fort Myers, back when Deion Sanders still played Pop Warner football. Those who followed him would be indebted, whether they knew it or not, to Johnnie Wright.

5 Wright and Wrong

When Deion Sanders was born in 1967, Johnnie Wright was approaching his ninth birthday, preparing for his foray into youth football.

In 1969, most of Dunbar's future NFL players were infants or had yet to be born. Deion Sanders turned two. Jevon Kearse was seven years from being born. Sandra Smith, whose four children would include future Tampa Bay Buccaneer Earnest Graham, attended the old Dunbar High School. She transferred to North Fort Myers High following the 1969 court order to desegregate schools. When Smith, her classmates, and their neighbors boarded their school buses, they were transported several miles away to the previously white-only high schools at Cypress Lake, Fort Myers, North Fort Myers High, and, later, Riverdale, Cape Coral, and Mariner High.

The children of Fort Myers had no local NFL players after whom to model themselves until 1982, when Wright suited up for the Baltimore Colts.

Wright, born on September 13, 1958, grew up on Highland Avenue, adjacent to the corner grocery store his father owned and operated until shortly before his death in 1999. Johnnie Wright had one brother and five sisters, and they lived in a three-bedroom home. Their father hailed from Georgia and their mother from South Carolina. Wright grew up playing football just as the youth sport spread throughout urban Fort Myers. By his senior season at Cypress Lake High School in 1975, Wright had grown to six feet, one inch, and weighed 190 pounds. He rushed for 1,391 yards and 8 touchdowns, becoming the first "megarecruit" from Fort Myers. His college choices came down to Florida, Florida State, and South Carolina, and he visited all three schools.

"It was just starting back then," Wright said of college football recruiting as it is known today. "They weren't really recruiting this area back then. I got about thirty letters from different colleges. I even got a letter from Harvard and the Naval Academy. I had a B minus.

"I couldn't go to Harvard."

Wright went to South Carolina. His mother had roots there, and the coaching staff convinced him he could play there as a freshman. One other aspect sealed the deal.

"When I went to visit, they reminded me of the Rebels," Wright said of his former Pop Warner program, the Fort Myers Rebels. That same program eventually developed and molded Deion Sanders and a host of other future NFL players. "The way they got fired up for a game? That's why I went there."

Warren Williams Sr., a Fort Myers native, a 1955 Dunbar High School graduate, and the father of former Pittsburgh Steelers running back Warren Williams Jr., told anyone who would listen that Johnnie Wright was the best college football player of the 1970s. Another man, one who knows a thing or two about star power, seconded the notion.

"He was big-time," said George Rogers, who won the 1980 Heisman Trophy, college football's highest honor. Rogers and Wright were recruited together at South Carolina. They were teammates.

"I was getting the ball as much as he was, and he was getting it as much as I was," Rogers said.

During the 1978 season as sophomores, the six-foot, two-inch, 220-pound Rogers rushed for 1,006 yards on 176 carries (5.7 yards per carry). Wright, then listed at six feet, one inch, and 200 pounds, also received 176 carries, which he took for 903 yards (5.1 yards per carry). Fans nicknamed the duo "George Left and Johnnie Wright."

Injury intervened. In his junior year, Wright tore the medial collateral ligament in his right knee, and he sat out the 1979 season. By the time he came back in 1980, Rogers, a junior, had positioned himself as a Heisman Trophy candidate, rushing for 1,681 yards the season before. The coaching staff moved Wright to fullback. He helped block for Rogers, who ran for 1,781 yards and lived up to the preseason hype, winning the Heisman Trophy and solidifying himself as a South Carolina sensation.

"Once he got hurt and had to sit out a year, I was getting the ball a majority of the time," said Rogers, who conceded that he probably would not have won the Heisman had Wright not been injured because they would have been sharing the workload. Rogers conceded something else: that if he had suffered the injury instead of Wright, Wright probably could have won the Heisman Trophy instead. Their offensive line dominated, and Wright could run that well.

"That's why you keep looking in front of you, so you don't have to look back," Rogers said. "I take pride in what I did. He ran hard, and I did too."

Playing football as a child helped steer Wright clear of trouble. And from the 1950s onward, trouble always seemed to be raging on the streets of Fort Myers.

"When I was a kid, the drugs were big," Wright said. "They'd be hanging out in the street, selling it and everything. Anderson Avenue, it was the hot place for drugs. Our streets were a lot tougher back then. I used football to stay out of trouble and stay off the streets. But if anything, I dedicated too much to football."

Wright made it to the NFL, but he didn't stay there long. His NFL career failed following one season's worth of special teams work. He received just 2 touches on offense, 1 carry for a 3-yard gain, and 1 reception for 12 yards while with the Baltimore Colts. Wright played the 1984 season with the Washington Federals of the United States Football League. He then enlisted in the U.S. Army, serving from 1986 until 1990. He spent two of those years stationed in Germany and two years at Fort Bliss in Texas. He fell nine credit hours short of earning his college degree in interdisciplinary studies. By the time he returned to Fort Myers in the mid-1990s, Wright had limited opportunities for employment. He found fulfillment in returning to high school football fields with stints as an assistant coach at Cypress Lake, Riverdale, Charlotte, and Lehigh Senior High Schools.

Although playing football kept Wright out of trouble as a youth, coaching the sport did not do the same for him as an adult. Wright developed bipolar disorder and suffered violent mood swings. He became addicted to cocaine.

The addiction and the mood swings cost him his football coaching jobs and contact with his three daughters and his sisters. They led him to lose touch with his mother, Rosella Wright. December 2, 2005, was the darkest day in Wright's life, the day he finally crossed the line. Wright flew into a rage as he was sitting in his mother's home. When his mother came in, Wright stood.

"You owe me thirty dollars," Johnnie said in a tone that filled the room with tension.

Rosella Wright assured her son she already had given him the money. She would end up giving him more. Her son, then forty-seven and still built like a hulk of a man, balled up his fists and threatened her. Then he grabbed her, forcing her outside. He gripped her by the neck—this is all according to the testimony she gave to the Lee County Sheriff's Office and later confirmed by both mother and son in interviews—and threw her into a shallow drainage ditch at the end of their driveway, injuring her left wrist. When the assault ended, Rosella Wright handed her son fifty dollars. Then she called the police, who found Johnnie Wright sitting on the front porch. Officer Albert Antonini told Wright he was under arrest and ordered him to place his hands behind his back. Wright refused. As Antonini and another officer then approached him, Wright further disgraced himself. He stood and swung at the second officer. The struggle spilled into the front yard. Antonini punched Wright three times in the right thigh. They were on the ground, rolling, punching, and elbowing one another. Antonini used his Taser gun to no initial effect. One prong hit Wright. The other lodged in his shirt. Wright rose and ran. He did not get far. Antonini fired the Taser gun again, this time hitting Wright in the upper chest, forcing him to collapse. Only then were Antonini and his partner able to handcuff Wright and arrest him.

Johnnie Wright spent a few months in jail. Rosella Wright filed a restraining order against her son, prohibiting him from coming within one hundred feet of her. Then Johnnie Wright pulled a disappearing act of sorts. Whispers and rumors swirled that he had been placed into a mental health facility. His drug problems and arrest record prohibited him from working with high school football players again. The old guard of Dunbar lost track of him. Not even Warren Williams Sr., who knew everything and everybody from Dunbar, knew how to find Wright.

Wright turned out to be one of the toughest people for me to find while I was researching this book. Within a week after asking Williams for help in tracking down Wright, however, I received a note from Wright in the mail at my office. He had typed the note, giving me his phone number.

Wright, in fact, had sought outpatient treatment at a mental health clinic in North Fort Myers. He volunteered at a homeless shelter and at a secondhand clothing thrift store. He rented a house in Pine Manor, another Fort Myers low-income neighborhood often referred to by its nickname of Crime Manor, where we met for our interview.

By 2010, five years after her son threw her to the ground, Rosella Wright said she would be open to talking to him again. Despite the restraining order she filed against him, she expected her son to make contact with her first. "He's the one who wronged me," she said. "He's the one who needs to apologize. I'm open to him calling me. But I'm not ready for him to be a part of my life yet. He has my phone number. He knows how to reach me."

Told of this, Wright said he didn't know his mother would be open to him calling her.

"I think I'll call her," Johnnie Wright said. He mended the fences with his mother before she died in November of 2012.

Asked why he was open to sharing his story, Johnnie Wright, who seemed so shy and so bashful and so incapable of violence, responded: "Because I'm proud of what I did in football. I don't want people to forget what I did."

Before Prime

Deion Sanders said he never knew of Johnnie Wright, but he did follow the path of Eric Riley, the third Dunbar-raised player to reach an NFL training camp.

Riley, born on August 15, 1962, grew up not far from Deion Sanders's grandmother's house. He attended Fort Myers High School, graduating in 1980 before moving on to Florida State University, graduating in 1985. Riley's time in college coincided with Sanders's time in high school.

Riley grew up in Southward Village, housing projects that were built in the 1960s. Adjacent to Southward Village were a recreation center, outdoor basketball courts, and youth baseball fields that later would be called the STARS Complex. Across the street lived Hattie Mims, grandmother of Deion Sanders.

"I grew up right there on Willard Street," Riley said. "I used to hang out at the rec center and play in that big tree over there at the end of Willard and I think it was Pauldo. It was a big tree there. The other half of that building was the office for the clinic. Those were good times back then."

Riley, the sixth child, had two brothers and five sisters. His father worked as a shrimper in Jacksonville and eventually moved to the Florida Keys. Eric Riley's mother, Flossie Mae Riley, worked for the Fort Myers Housing Authority for many years, long enough to have a building named in her honor.

"My parents separated when I came along," Riley said. "I kind of grew up without my dad. There were so many of us."

Riley turned to Fort Myers High School football coach Sam Sirianni and a young assistant coach named Joe Hampton for guidance.

"Those coaches deserve a lot of credit," Riley said. "A lot of those males who are working in the school system deserve a lot of credit for being good influences."

Had he not loved football, Riley said, he could have gotten caught up in the drug trade. "I had friends who used to hang out and do that stuff," Riley said. "They used to sniff dye back then. Kids were doing that. I had some crazy buddies back then. I was known as an athlete. I used to pass them every day. They'd be hanging out by that tree that I used to play at a lot. We'd chat a little bit. They were doing that stuff. They knew that I was going to go running, and they were respectful of me."

That type of respect developed into a code within Dunbar. The drug pushers would encourage rising young athletes to steer clear of the drug trade and would shelter rising athletes from trouble. Riley experienced this code first. He also noticed the repercussions from desegregation. Had he been born a decade earlier, he would have remembered drinking out of separate water fountains from his white contemporaries.

"I left Willard Street and went to the ball field at ten years old, played for the Mighty Mite Jets," Riley said. "We practiced across from the old Coca Cola plant."

That plant, where Coca Cola bottled sodas in the 1970s, burned down when a gang of white and Hispanic teenagers from Riverdale High School, nicknamed the "Lords of Chaos," set fire to it in April 1996. A CVS pharmacy later was built on the site.

"I was riding my bike out there from Willard, and I remember going through a neighborhood," Riley said. "And a little kid, couldn't have been older than six or seven years old, saw me."

That little kid called Riley a racial epithet.

"I remember thinking, 'Where the heck did he learn that word from?'" Riley said. "I remember being fourteen or fifteen. When I was younger, there were some serious issues. We used to walk home from football practice, and I remember being chased. I remember kids in our neighborhood, on Edison and Ford Streets. These were older kids. They would throw rocks at cars. They would look, and if it were a white person, they would throw a rock. That had to do with the racial tension. To this day, my mom, she didn't know I was present at those unfortunate, crazy situations."

Flossie Mae Riley had a tremendous impact on her son. Her unflagging work ethic motivated him. She worked full-time for the housing authority, eventually becoming its director. In the early years, she found part-time work at convenience stores. She always encouraged her son to stay in sports. Alexander Riley, one of Eric's older brothers, also played a big role.

"He was two years older than me, but he seemed like he was much, much older than me with his influence," Riley said. "He always said, 'If you want to be good in sports, you can't drink.' At a young age, that stuck in my head. People don't realize how tough and hard-nosed he was. He just didn't have that natural, fluid, athletic body control and speed that I had. He tore up his knee and decided he didn't want to play football in college."

Eric Riley had big dreams then. He wanted to play in the NFL and intercept passes thrown by Joe Namath or Roger Staubach. He wanted to play against O. J. Simpson, back when Simpson was known only for his football abilities.

Riley only sniffed the dream. The Denver Broncos drafted him in the eighth round in 1985, but he never made a regular-season NFL roster.

"It was an experience," Riley said. "I never really reached the dream. I never got out of the blocks. But it was a great experience to get drafted and to be in NFL camps. I was with the Broncos, and I was with the Rams when they were still in L.A. and still had Eric Dickerson. I helped my mom get a home. She was able to buy it outright. That helped our family, coming from nothing. I definitely felt good to be able to do that."

Another player also caught a glimpse of the dream.

Donald Dupreist Ellis, also known as "Donald Duck," or simply "Duck," spent a large chunk of his childhood in Southward Village, also known as the Old Projects. Born on March 18, 1966, Ellis also spent a lot of time in a home on Bassie Court, part of Left Corner.

Left Corner, over time, would come to exemplify the drug trade and culture that still pervades Dunbar.

"Once you're considered part of Left Corner, it never gets out of you," Ellis said. "People from Left Corner . . . you may move out of Left Corner, but you'll always end up back there. On Left Corner, somebody is always going to bring up football or sports."

Ellis and Shedrick Diggs, also of Left Corner, were friends and high school football teammates. They went 10–0 in 1983 at Cypress Lake High.

"In high school, my biggest worry was getting to school on time," Ellis said. "Shed's mom bought him a car his senior year. I call her Aunt Jenny. She's not my blood aunt, but because of my relationship with Shed, she's always been in my life, so no one can tell me she's not my aunt.

"Aunt Jenny bought Shed a car. A yellow Grenada. I'll never forget that car. No one ever rode in that car except me and Shed. Nobody. Those were my worries. Getting to school on time. Seeing if I could get into a girl's panties. Shed and I were sixteen years old. We could go and get into any club in the downtown area. And we would go."

They would go until traveling their separate ways, Diggs to the University of South Carolina as a linebacker and Ellis to the University of Miami.

Ellis became a go-to player, both in games and during practices. Ellis and future Pro Football Hall of Famer Michael Irvin were wide receivers on the Miami scout team as freshmen.

"A week before the Florida game, the starting corner got hurt," Ellis said. Coach Jimmy Johnson called Ellis into his office.

"Keep in mind, I hadn't played defensive back at all in college, and he told me, he says, 'We as a coaching staff, we want to switch you over to cornerback. One reason you were highly recruited is because you were a defensive back, and you could play wide receiver. We feel like you can make the change and be a big contributor at cornerback.'"

After one day of practice at cornerback, Johnson named Ellis a starter for the next game, less than five days away.

"He was smart," said Irvin, who attended St. Thomas Aquinas High in Fort Lauderdale. "He understood the game. Man, I think about all them dudes who didn't make it who came from the same places as us. I saw plenty of dudes like Donnie. I always said he could have been a movie star if he would have made it. He was a pretty black man, he spoke well, and he could play. He had great feet, great change of direction and great hands.

"He was a ladies' man. Maybe that was his undoing."

A devastating right-knee injury began Ellis's undoing. It happened on the next-to-last play during a game against Florida State his junior year, following a sensational sophomore season that put him on the map as a cover cornerback.

Ellis played in pain through that 1987 season, one in which the Hurricanes won the NCAA national title. The coaches told Ellis he could start, because playing at 70 to 75 percent health, he still performed better than the cornerbacks who were playing at 100 percent. Trainers would drain the knee on Tuesdays and again on Fridays, the day before games.

"It just took a toll on me," Ellis said. "On our team, we had so much love and admiration for each other. There's just something about that era. I was part of starting that dynasty."

More than thirty years after playing, Ellis refused to watch the Hurricanes play on TV. The physical pain in his knee caused him to walk with a limp. His NFL prospects were long gone, along with the cartilage in his right knee. After finishing football, Ellis stayed in the Miami area, working for a company that sold computer products. In 1996, his girlfriend Gina died.

"That was the last straw," Ellis said. "I had nothing else left in this world. That was the only woman who truly loved me after the injury. She's the only one who stuck with me."

Ellis spiraled into a depression. He became a vagabond, living in Clewiston and Orlando in Florida and Houston and New Orleans, always on the move and always looking for work. He had jobs as a restaurant cook, delivery driver, and furniture salesman.

"Prozac. Zoloft. Trazodone," Ellis said. "All the crap they had me on, at one point I was a walking zombie because I was always medicated. I was always on something. Wherever I went, there was always a facility that would help you with your meds."

Upon arriving in a new city, Ellis sought drug clinics willing to treat those without health insurance. Ellis turned to alcohol for solace as well.

"It got to the point where, if I didn't have a drink, I understand how some alcoholics get the shakes if they don't have a drink, and all it took was a sip to stop the shakes," Ellis said. "The alcohol was always a crutch."

Ellis said his spiral into alcoholism and dabbling in drugs did not begin until more than ten years after leaving college, after Gina's death. His arrest record began then as well: using controlled substances, violating his probation, loitering, driving with a revoked driver's license, loitering (again), obstructing justice, failure to appear in court, and finally, in August 2010, felony cocaine possession, for which he was released on bond.

Afterward, Ellis said, he kept himself clean. He spent many of his days near Dunbar at the Touched By Angels hair salon, where his sister and his mother worked. Ellis sought refuge there and at the homes of other caring family members, the people who always have loved him unconditionally and who helped him to stop searching for something he could never find.

With Ellis's mother getting older and his son struggling with legal issues related to his arrest for selling marijuana, Don Ellis pulled himself out of his personal gutter and returned home for good.

"My mother and my children," Ellis said. "What kind of made me snap out of it was basically that my children need me. My mother is getting older. Her physical condition isn't what it used to be. You've got to get out of your own shit, man, because these people need you. That's what triggered it. That's what made me snap out of it.

"It helped me get back to a place of sanity. At one point, I was insane. Going place to place to place to place but never finding nothing. I've come to believe that being insane is doing the same thing over and over and over again, expecting a different result. You've got to be crazy to walk across the street ten times and get hit by the same bus. Ten times! Something has to be wrong with you to keep walking by that same house and getting bit by the same dog.

"That's insanity, to keep going by that house, knowing that dog is going to bite you. Something has to be mentally wrong with you, not to change your life."

Although Ellis changed his life, one thing never would change.

"I will never get over Gina," Ellis said. "That will always, always be a thorn in my heart."

Ellis had a longtime fan in fellow Dunbar resident and University of Miami teammate Warren Williams Jr.

"Let me tell you something," Williams said. "Donnie was the best pure defensive back. Donnie was the best cover man, and a physical corner. Donnie had that knee injury. They shot him up and let him play and ruined him. I love Donnie."

Just as the love for his mother brought Ellis back home, the love for both of his parents brought Williams back to Dunbar. Born on July 29, 1965, to Rosa Lee and Warren Williams Sr., Williams preceded Deion Sanders by two years at North Fort Myers High School and competed against Ellis when he played for the Cypress Lake Panthers.

Williams lured more college football recruiters to Fort Myers. The six-foot, 203-pound running back played for five seasons with the Pittsburgh Steelers in 1988–92 after being drafted in the sixth round as the No. 155 overall pick. He had 251 career carries for 1,191 yards (4.7 yards per carry) and 8 touchdowns. He caught 38 passes for 339 yards and 2 touchdowns.

Williams also played for the 1987 national championship Miami Hurricanes team. He did so after honing his athletic skills in the driveway of his Pauldo Street home. The Williams family had a basketball goal outside. As soon as Williams was old enough to stand, he shot baskets in that driveway. He learned to play football in the front yard, which consisted of just a narrow strip of grass. The games spilled into the street. One of Warren's uncles used to get aggressive with the kids. He threw the ball hard enough to knock Warren onto his backside. This prepared Williams for his future as a Pittsburgh Steelers special teams standout, tackling or blocking during kick and punt returns.

"I was always the alternate for the Pro Bowl, for like five straight years," Williams said, bringing up an NFL rival and one of the game's all-time best special teams players with the Buffalo Bills. "Steve Tasker. I put him on his butt every game. When we played him, always in the AFC Championship Game, I put his ass on the ground. Every game, you can look at it from 1989 to 1993, the first play of every game, I knocked somebody down. Every game."

Williams knocked people down in football but did his best to lift up others in Dunbar. Williams would go on to have seven children. They grew up as the NFL transformed from a Sunday-afternoon diversion into a career goal.

"There wasn't a football player I emulated in this community," Williams said of his own childhood. "I liked Eric Riley. He was a friend of the family. His sister is like a sister to me. Three years ahead of me. I liked Johnnie Wright. I followed his career when he was at South Carolina. But the recruiters didn't come to this area. We didn't even think about the NFL. I didn't think I could go to the pros until after my freshman year in college. I was with one of my buddies, and he said, 'Hey, we're going to the NFL.'

"I wanted to go to college. I didn't know if I would go to college for sports or music. I played the tuba. I love music. It's still a passion of mine. I still have a lot of old cassette tapes and six or seven hundred CDs. I like old rhythm and blues, believe it or not, Motown.

"My mom influenced me. She was a Christian lady. There were a lot of things we couldn't do that other kids could do. The television went off at nine o'clock on Sundays. Friday and Saturday night, we used to play all the old black movies. My mom and my dad, they were hard-working people, and they set the best example of anyone. If you work hard, you can do anything."

Rosa Lee Williams, known for her skills as a soul food cook, worked for several years at Lee Memorial Hospital, as did Connie Knight, the mother of Deion Sanders, which was how Williams and Sanders first met. Warren Williams Sr. owned a liquor store and also sold auto parts.

The strong bond Williams Jr. had with his parents kept him from looking outside of Florida when it came to choosing a college. That bond also kept him from getting into drugs.

"I had like seventy-five different scholarship offers to different places," said Williams, who played at Miami under coach Howard Schnellenberger during the infancy of a college football dynasty. Bernie Kosar, Vinny Testaverde, and Steve Walsh, all future NFL quarterbacks, played at Miami during Williams Jr.'s time there.

When Williams finished playing professional football, he stayed in the game, working for the NFL as part of the league's then-new uniform police. Williams would sit in a stadium box with binoculars, looking for and then recommending fines for players who violated the league's uniform rules on game day.

"Socks down. Shirts out," Williams said. "They didn't want a Dennis Rodman situation in the NFL."

After a few years of doing that, Williams returned to the house in which he lived as a child. He lived the early part of his life at 2800 Anderson Avenue, right across the street from an old funeral home. The family moved to Pauldo Street in 1967, a house they would stay in for more than forty years and counting.

Their neighbors were educators. By the mid-1980s, however, drugs increasingly were creeping into Dunbar.

"That was during the time of Larry White and Ronnie Tape," Williams said of two men who would be convicted of drug dealing and sent to prison. "And beyond them, there were tons and tons of kingpins. But we still had a community that cared. News travels fast. If somebody was killed, you could find out before the cops did."

Despite Tape's transgressions, Williams described Tape as more like Robin Hood than Boyz in the Hood.

"He bought uniforms for some of the sports teams," Williams said. "He'd give needy kids presents for Christmas. He did a lot of positive things. It wasn't always negative. He helped a lot of businesses in Dunbar. There were a lot of things he did that were positive. I still like him."

After Tape went to prison, the dynamics of drug dealing in Dunbar changed. Instead of having a few leaders at the top, there were fragmented pockets of dealers scattered across Lee County. Turf wars contributed to a record twenty-four homicides in 2012 in Fort Myers.

"It's a bunch of renegades in this community now," Williams said. "Nobody knows who is killing who."

By 2014, Williams had left the NFL behind him. He said he fit in fine in Fort Myers, working as a night-shift supervisor at the Walmart off Colonial Boulevard, near I-75. He felt at peace being in his hometown, forever connected to the many athletes who preceded and followed him.

"I love my parents, and I love this community," Williams said. "I don't hide. I go into this community where people see me. I paid my dues. I live where I live comfortably. I can do things for my parents. If I want to take off and go somewhere, I can do it. I've been blessed."

Tape's Time

Ronnie Lee Tape, as a sixth-grader trying to win a two-mile run, started off sprinting as if he were running the 100-yard dash.

"You know what happened next, right?" Tape said.

As he slowed to a jog on his way from the Fort Myers Country Club to Fort Myers High School's Edison Stadium, he could only watch as the field of runners passed him.

Gerald Copeland, Tape's physical education teacher at Fort Myers Middle Academy, encouraged Tape.

"You just don't know how to pace yourself, Ronnie," Copeland told him.

The lack of pacing led Tape to trouble. More than forty years later, Tape had spent almost half his life in prison. Even so, by April 2013, Tape did not look like a drug dealer who once had received a life sentence for selling crack cocaine, living in an 8' × 10' cell with one to two cellmates. When the fifty-four-year-old emerged from the doorway within the minimum security prison in Coleman, Florida, and into the visitors' room, there were only two telltale signs as to the fate that befell him.

Number one, Tape wore an army-green prisoner uniform. Number two, Tape entered a room full of about one hundred prisoners, who were talking to friends and family members on a Monday morning.

Tape looked healthy and trim, not overly fit or fat for his age. He continued his favorite exercise of running, only from within the barbed-wire complex, where the scent of fresh-cut grass mixed with the stench of sweat from the daily basketball games played outside on a concrete court. Tape wore a pair of eyeglasses and had long dreadlocks that gave him the aura of a retired reggae star.

Born on January 23, 1959, Tape grew up aspiring to be a professional in music, not in football or other sports. The musical roots were handed down from his father. Tape favored jazz and popular rock. He learned to play the drums, keyboard, and bass guitar and how to program beats and operate a studio mixing board in a recording studio.

During the mid-1980s, Tape traveled often to Hollywood, California, where a friend connected him with Little Richard's producer, Bumps Blackwell. The album with Tape's band, Slip-n-Slide, never got recorded, but Tape often stayed in Los Angeles. He leased a six-bedroom home with a pool in Beverly Hills, just down the street from Burt Bacharach, the acclaimed pianist, composer, and music producer who worked with Elvis Costello, Dionne Warwick, Dusty Springfield, and Dr. Dre.

Tape also connected with Berry and Terry Gordy, the sons of famed music producer Berry Gordy. The Gordy brothers, whose father worked with the Jackson 5, the Supremes, the Temptations, Stevie Wonder, and many others, took an interest in Slip-n-Slide. They liked Tape until a defecting band member informed the Gordys of Tape's secret life back home in Fort Myers. They soon learned Tape's truth: he was dealing drugs. They dropped their talks with Tape, who then regrouped.

The mid-1980s were kind and thrilling to Tape, who relocated his recording studio from the California home he had been leasing to a building he remodeled on Melrose Avenue. He installed state-of-the-art equipment, including an $800,000 soundboard that later would become part of his undoing. Tape paid for it in cash, and that caught the attention of federal agents back in Fort Myers. Tape began to meet more of the music industry's top producers, enabling him to cross paths with Michael Jackson, Eddie Murphy, Sheila E., Herb Alpert, Jermaine Jackson, and a host of Paramount Pictures executives among other Hollywood power players of the era. Lionel Richie remixed his song "Don't Stop" in Tape's studio. Vanessa Williams, in her infancy as an entertainer, visited that studio as a prospective client but never recorded there.

Tape had his hands in real estate as well. He once purchased a $1.2 million home in West Hollywood. For his twenty-sixth birthday, he bought a showroom Rolls Royce. He met real estate investors who taught him how to buy high-end homes in Beverly Hills, remodel them, and then flip them for at least $300,000 or more in profits, all with bank financing. Tape sold a $4.2 million home in Bel Air and received 6 percent of the sale.

All the while, Tape maintained his drug-dealing business in Fort Myers. Tape didn't just sell drugs. He had amassed, in his mid-twenties, one of the largest cocaine and crack cocaine distribution networks in the nation, headquartered in then-tiny Fort Myers, where the sprawl south of U.S. 41 had yet to connect with Naples and where the college football recruiting machine had yet to truly take hold. Deion Sanders was still a half year away from his high school graduation.

Tape had his accomplices manage the drug trade during his trips to California, but he took many a red-eye flight home to oversee his empire on the streets of Dunbar.

"I was able to avoid any serious violence, because in the beginning, I set the tone by going after anyone that robbed my workers," Tape said.

Tape or someone close to him would beat up the rival dealer if he had to. Then Tape would turn around and befriend him, employing him in his ring.

"That gained respect back then, so they basically left my workers alone," Tape said. "Plus, I would give him a job if he wanted one. There was very little violence back in the day. Dealers were more focused on making money."

When Tape peaked as a moneymaker, he had amassed an arsenal not of weapons but of high-end cars. At the time of his arrest, Tape's fleet of cars included a 1981 Cadillac, a 1984 Datsun 300ZX, a 1982 Jaguar, a 1983 Jaguar, a leased Mercedes 560 SEL, a Mercedes 190E, and that 1985 showroom-model Rolls Royce, according to courthouse records detailing Tape's case.

The court records revealed Tape's bank account information as well. In 1983, he had $24,040 in deposits. The numbers rose from there: $133,759 in 1984, $762,328 in 1985, and $575,145 in 1986.

And that was only what Tape had in the bank. He dealt mostly in cash. During the mid-1980s, about $100,000 in cash would change hands every day in Dunbar. Tape estimated that during 1985 he made about $20,000 cash per day.

Tape's drug dealing all began at one of the few places of legal business in Dunbar, the since-removed Star Service Station on Anderson Avenue. Tape graduated from Riverdale High School in 1978. He once got suspended at Riverdale for fighting in what he described as a race riot in the school cafeteria. Tape picked up a chair and smashed it onto a white student, who was threatening to throttle Tape as well.

From Riverdale, Tape began working at the gas station, making about $350 a week, plus an occasional bonus.

With savings from his legally earned salary and bonus money, Tape bought his first new car, a showroom-floor 1979 Z28 Camaro, maroon with black and gold stripes.

In 1979, construction of Interstate 75 began. The four-lane, divided highway had no stoplights and a speed limit of 75 miles an hour. It shaped Dunbar in two significant ways. It gave much easier access for college football coaches to recruit in Southwest Florida. It also gave Tape and other drug dealers a faster way to transport their products.

That same year, Tape began dealing drugs. In selling cocaine, Tape became a user. Soon, he couldn't make the payments on his beloved Camaro because he spent too much of his money on using his own product. The Camaro ended up being repossessed. The cocaine gave Tape a surge in confidence, but he knew he needed to kick his growing addiction if he wanted to control the drugs versus the drugs controlling him.

Tape said he began using the drug only to test it for its purity. He continued selling ten-dollar bags of cocaine on the streets of Dunbar, hand to hand. As his profits grew, so did his connections to suppliers in

Miami, Jamaica, and Colombia. Tape began to get other people to work the streets for him. His product began to take over the streets, where he met resistance from other drug dealers who had been entrenched in the area. But Tape and his team of workers stood their ground. They continued to overcome their competitors by bringing in a bigger and better product. By 1983–84, Tape's drug business had taken off. He employed even more workers and expanded to the Tampa Bay area.

This is when Tape's jet-setting to Los Angeles began, and when it did, it opened Tape's eyes to Dunbar's destitution and its lack of businesses. Tape said he made plans to eventually drop the drug dealing. He used much of his drug-dealing profits to begin buying land off Anderson Avenue. He also bought a nightclub from a friend. The Phase II Lounge had a swimming pool that Tape had transformed into an aquarium for exotic fish, placing a glass dance floor on top of it. It had a venue for teenagers to get together on one side and for adults to party on the other.

"I didn't really want the nightclub," Tape said. "I bought it as a favor to a friend."

What Tape really wanted was for Dunbar to have a grocery store, chain restaurants, and other businesses. He envisioned a shopping center, and he began to plan twenty-two places of business, including a two-screen movie theater and a bank.

"I did the studies," Tape said. "We had the demographics."

Sitting in that Coleman prison visiting room, Tape pointed to imaginary spots on a white table.

"You had downtown here," Tape said, pointing to one spot representing downtown Fort Myers. "You had I-75 here. We had the people. Once the shopping center was built, I was going after franchises like McDonald's, Burger King, KFC, and others to create jobs in the Dunbar community off Anderson Avenue."

Tape hired an architect to get the project rolling. Fort Myers city councilwoman Veronica Shoemaker soon got wind of Tape's plan. That resulted in an article in the *Fort Myers News-Press* soliciting developers and offering incentives to build the shopping center. Three developers submitted their bids, plans, and proposals. Tape won the bid.

"I don't know why I had to go through all of that," Tape said. "Maybe the city was trying to save face for neglecting the Dunbar community for all these years."

While Tape's long-term vision of a prosperous Dunbar seemed noble, his short-term, disruptive, and destructive business of selling crack cocaine caught the attention of the federal government.

In 1987, the federal government dispatched prosecutor Douglas Frazier to Fort Myers.

"I came down here to open the office," said Frazier, who started that job at age thirty-seven. By age sixty-two, he had advanced to a U.S. district judge of the Twentieth Judicial Circuit. "I was the first federal prosecutor here. I had an office at the old courthouse across the street. There was no security. Congressman Connie Mack, the elder (and the grandson of the Hall of Fame baseball manager), was a congressman and not a senator yet. He was in the building. And the FBI had a couple of agents.

"There were several things going on. One was the smuggling going on in Everglades City. Two, there was the crack cocaine epidemic here. I came from New Orleans, and we never really saw crack cocaine. We saw PCP, cocaine, and heroin.

"Fort Myers was kind of unique. The quantities and the quality of the crack cocaine here were incredible. People came here from all over the South to get it. It was a geographic phenomenon in some respect. You had the proximity of Miami with powder cocaine. They could transport it across Alligator Alley or across U.S. 41. You had a distribution network in the black community that was based on cocaine and heroin, boy and girl. They would wrap it in foil. The point was, the way they did the math, the way they cut up the drug, they had moneymaking capability.

"Geographically, it all came together here in a perfect storm."

Tape said he did not fully realize the harm he did to his community. He just wanted to make money. As a young child and as a young man, dealing drugs seemed the most logical way to do it. There were very few businesses in Dunbar. Those who grew up in the neighborhood and attained college degrees and successful careers as doctors and lawyers or as professional athletes rarely returned to the community. Positive role models existed in teachers and in law enforcement officers, but there were not enough of them. They were outnumbered and overwhelmed.

"At the beginning, I couldn't see the devastation of the Dunbar community, because I was born in it," Tape said. "So that was a normal way of life to me, seeing the community that way. I wasn't blinded by the money. The problem existed way before me, and it still continues to exist to this day.

"My reasoning was that alcohol ruined my mother's life, therefore I figured that drugs were no different or worse than alcohol. That type of thinking is what blinded me."

Tape, who insisted he wanted good for his community, had his eyes shut to the damage he did to his hometown. The federal government did not. On May 25, 1988, the federal government came down hard on Tape and his accomplices, charging Tape with nine counts of violating federal narcotic laws with intent to distribute and distribution of cocaine base and crack cocaine.

"We brought in undercover agents from Milwaukee and St. Petersburg," Frazier said of the period just prior to when the arrests were made. "We put together a combination of tax evasion and a drug indictment."

The feds never found Tape in possession of the drugs. They didn't need to. About a dozen of Tape's accomplices were given plea-bargain deals, lesser sentences, in return for their testimony against Tape.

"When we did the takedown, we took down everybody," Frazier said. "We set up out at the old pistol and rifle range, off Anderson, almost to the interstate. We set up there. Everybody went out and hit these people. Ronnie left that night. He had a Mercedes. He got away. Then we put all of our guys after him. They started tracking him. We got a tip."

Tape recalled seeing a shooting star on the night he was arrested. A tip led law enforcement to a trailer park near Sanibel Island. An officer with a K-9 unit found Tape, who recalled hiding in the bedroom closet of a trailer. The deputies broke open the unlocked door. Tape held his hands outside of the closet, acknowledging his defeat. Tape said after the officers cuffed him, they let the German shepherd bite him in the leg, in the arm, and almost where it counts—between his legs. According-ing to numerous media accounts, then-sheriff Frank Wanicka fed the dog ice cream for dinner as a reward.

On April 18, 1989, Tape received a life sentence, which was reduced on June 3, 2008, to 360 months (thirty years). Tape had an estimated release date of September 24, 2014, which moved up to November 2013 after he completed a ten-month drug-education class. In between, both of Tape's parents died, and his seven children produced twenty-one grandchildren. Tape would see some of them in prison visits, and he followed their lives from afar. While in prison, he plotted one of the first things he would do upon his release: take his family to the beach.

"It's a sad thing for Mr. Tape at thirty or thirty-one years of age and with an engaging personality as shown to me by the witnesses who ap-peared here, a heart that is almost as big as his wallet, which was quite substantial as a result of his dealing in drugs—in the community that is just crying out for some kind of relief from this," Judge Lee Gagliardi said at the Tape's sentencing in 1989. "It is a tragic story to see people in that neighborhood, whether they are on drugs or not, I don't know, but they are certainly affected by it over there. And it is a sad thing, and it's not going to get any better.

"I would like to think this particular case was going to wipe out drugs in Dunbar, but I am sure that there are others willing to take the gamble that Mr. Tape took in enriching himself, because the profits to be real-ized from this illegal sale are one of the great crises in our country.

"We are not going to solve it in the courts, unfortunately. But per-haps we can deter somebody from following this path. And that is what these sentencing guidelines are designed to do, to show that you shouldn't be involved in the first place. If you are involved in it, you are in trouble. And if you are caught and convicted, you are in even greater trouble. That's the sad story of this particular case, the case of Ronnie Tape and his associates."

On a bad day, Tape and his crew made $10,000. On Friday, payday, they would make $40,000. The temptation to deal was real. But so was serving the time for doing the crime.

Gagliardi wasn't finished.

"Unfortunately, [the Dunbar neighborhoods are] engulfed in poverty," Gagliardi said. "There are many fatherless, or at least unknown fathers, for the children who are there. It is just a sad story. And this is just a small microcosm of what is happening throughout the United States. Fort Myers is not a large place. It is too bad and sad that the first time I am confronted with it, I have to impose a life sentence to a thirty-year-old individual. I do it with regret but with no remorse, because the law is the law as it is.

"It is a shame that this capable talent wasn't better directed to the improvement of the Fort Myers neighborhood rather than to its ruin."

Tape held himself accountable for all of the accusations against him but for one: the "ruin" of Dunbar. His fellow citizens began their lives poor. Their parents began their lives poor. Their parents before them were the direct descendants of slaves. It takes money to make money, Tape said, which was what drew him to dealing drugs. The lack of assistance from the government, Tape said, only kept his community from rising from poverty.

"The leaders downtown, they don't know how to bring about a change to the Dunbar community," Tape said. "They are not providing a support system for the youth there. They are not allowing for the creation of businesses, let alone for the growth of them."

The Sentence of Walter Sutton

Just as Tape looked up to the drug dealers surrounding him as a young man, future NFL draft pick Walter Sutton looked up to Tape. While Tape had excelled in music at Riverdale High, Sutton, who is thirteen years younger than Tape, found his calling in sports.

John Quintier coached the Riverdale High School boys' basketball team in the mid-1980s and described Sutton as one of his standouts.

"He was just one of those gifted athletes," Quintier said. "He may not have been as all-around an athlete as Deion, but he had a lot of the same athletic skills that Deion had. He had tremendous speed. His jump shot would hang up there forever. It was like he was on springs when he played."

Sutton didn't have the academic fortitude to qualify for a Division I scholarship. At five foot ten, he did not have the height, either. He recalled his first day of basketball practice at Southwest State University (now Southwest Minnesota State University), an NCAA Division II school of about 3,500 students in Marshall, Minnesota. He hit about fifteen jump shots in a row, nothing but net. He started messing around, driving to the rim and doing 360-degree slam dunks. During the 1988–89 season, Sutton led the team with 14.6 points per game. The basketball coach kicked him off the team after a teammate accused Sutton of stealing shoes out of his locker. Sutton had done a lot of illegal things in his young life, but Sutton said stealing from a teammate wasn't one of them. Still, the fallout from the incident forced Sutton off the basketball team entering 1989.

"A lot of stuff was on my plate," Sutton said. "I had that attitude I had in Fort Myers. I just had so much athletic ability, but I never grew up."

The football coach invited Sutton to try out and run the 40-yard dash. He ran it in 4.32 seconds.

"The coached stopped what he was doing. He had never seen that," Sutton said. "This coach came in with this new scheme on offense. I had one of the best junior college quarterbacks in the country at the time throwing to me."

That open tryout changed everything.

"It definitely changed my life, that day," Sutton said. "It told me I had a gift. The coach told me, 'If you listen to me, I promise you I'll get you a shot in the NFL. You've got so much ability. If you just listen to me, I'll get you a shot.' He changed my whole thinking process in life."

Back on a football field for the first time since the youth level, Sutton rediscovered his greatness on the gridiron. He had played against Deion Sanders in the Fort Myers city league and then later at the Pop Warner level before rising through the high school ranks against Sanders in basketball. Sanders and Sutton did not know each other very well as young children. When they were teenagers, Deion's father lived with Sutton's mother for a while. He had no other place to stay. "I love that dude, man," Sanders said of Sutton, two decades later. When Sanders endured his divorce from his first wife, Carolyn Chambers, Sutton visited him in Cincinnati, saying what he could to help a childhood friend.

Sanders and Sutton had a few things in common when it came to athletics. They differed in that Sanders always worked on honing his skills, whether in football, basketball, baseball, or track. Sutton possessed similar speed to Sanders. He just didn't know how to harness it. In addition to the speed, he had a forty-two-inch vertical leap. Once Sutton joined the Southwest State football team, he began dedicating himself to learning the nuances of being a wide receiver, how to run crisp, clean routes, read opposing defenses, study passing patterns and formations. His life, he thought, had changed forever. He was eating, drinking, and breathing football. The efforts showed in his prolific statistics. As a junior for the Southwest State Mustangs in 1989, he caught 61 passes for 818 yards and 6 touchdowns. As a senior in the fall of 1990, he caught 61 passes for 687 yards and 7 touchdowns.

The Atlanta Falcons noticed. In the tenth round of the April 1991 NFL Draft, the Falcons selected Sutton. He became, after Johnnie Wright, Eric Riley, Warren Williams, Deion Sanders, and Richard Fain, the sixth player from Dunbar to be drafted by an NFL team.

There was just one problem.

Long before Sutton left for college in Minnesota, he had worked for Tape, selling cocaine as a teenager.

The previous September, Sutton pleaded guilty in United States District Court in Fort Myers to two counts of conspiracy to possess and distribute more than fifty grams of crack cocaine between 1986 and 1988, the height of the crack cocaine trade in the region. He was sentenced in February of 1991 to a nine-year prison term, with the judge allowing him to finish college before reporting to prison on January 28, 1992. Sutton never played a down in the NFL. He never even made it to training camp. Instead, he spent almost six years in prison for dealing drugs. In that pre-Internet era, the Falcons had no clue of the drugs in Sutton's past. Neither did the man who coached him.

"I was shocked when I found out that he was in that drug ring," Quintier said. "It's a shame. It ruined his life, because obviously, he could have gone far with the Falcons."

It didn't ruin Sutton's life, although it did alter it forever. Twenty years later, Sutton had made something of himself. He settled near Atlanta, where he founded his own music-producing company, Infrared

Entertainment. Sutton always wondered about a bunch of what-ifs, the biggest of which involved his youth football years.

What if, like Deion Sanders, he had played for the Fort Myers Rebels instead of the Tice Tigers? The Rebels had a better organization, one that stressed academics and that mentored the children, preparing them for success off the field as well as on it.

"In the eighth grade, I started playing for the Tice Tigers," Sutton said. "I was the quarterback." Sanders played running back for the Rebels. Sanders and Sutton got to know each other better then, and Sutton realized his biggest difference from Sanders. Sutton, whose father had divorced his mother and moved to Miami, later dying in a car accident, had no male role model in the home. His heroes were the drug pushers on the streets, the ones who drove flashy cars with rims, wore gold chains, and carried wads of cash.

Sanders had a number of prominent male role models, especially his youth football coach Dave Capel and his high school coach Ron Hoover. Sanders also had examples close to him of what not to do: using drugs in the case of his father, Mims Sanders, and drinking too much alcohol in the case of his stepfather, Willie Knight. Sanders also had a mother who realized the importance of athletics as an outlet in her son's life.

"As we moved on in life, and as we moved on in sports, he was getting the proper coaching," Sutton said. "That was the way it was. I don't think my mother was financially fit to put me into that [the mostly white and wealthier Rebels] system. That's not taking anything away from the Tice Tigers. That's just the way it was."

Sutton blamed his misdeeds and bad decisions on the environment around him. The environment around him stemmed from the community being isolated and segregated, even after the public schools were integrated in 1969.

"The Dunbar area was something else," Sutton said. "I blame a lot of what happened to me on the Dunbar area and the boys running around there. I used to blame it on those guys. The guys on the street were my role models. I didn't realize my true athletic ability."

Upon arriving at college, Sutton stood out from his teammates in speed and athletic ability but also in another way. He had lots of money, lots of clothes, and perhaps sixty pairs of sneakers. When involved with the drug trade, he made $20,000 to $30,000 a week.

"Money back then for me was not a problem," Sutton said. "There's something about the water in Fort Myers. You drank that water, you got caught up in it. I'm in a different station in life now."

Tape looked forward to making the transition from prison to the life outside again. When that day arrived, Tape's and Sutton's roles were reversed. Just as Tape mentored Sutton in the realm of the drug trade, Sutton offered to assist Tape in transitioning from prison life to law-abiding life.

"I'm now in a place in my life that he wants to be," Sutton said of Tape. "Ronnie Tape, he's my man. I'll do whatever I can to help him get here."

Tape's Transition

Tape followed the plight of Dunbar from prison. It wasn't hard. So many young men from Dunbar later joined Tape behind bars. Tape wished he could reach out to Dunbar's youth, to the children at Fort Myers Middle School and Caloosa Middle School, where he attended, to all of the children of Fort Myers and the rest of Southwest Florida.

While I was researching this book, two years passed from the time I first attempted to land a prison interview with Tape to the time he granted it. A conversation I had with his lawyer about the impact Tape could have on the youth of Fort Myers convinced him to change his mind and meet with me, sharing his story. Tape addressed the following comments to the youth of Fort Myers.

"I know that the environment and the obstacles you face in the area are horrible," Tape said. "But you must stay strong and not let all of the negative influences and negative environments overwhelm you. You must cling to any positivity you can find.

"Let the horrible environment and obstacles inspire you to want to do better and want better for yourself and others. Get a good education so that you can place yourself in a position to make a difference.

"I realize that kids today have access to a lot more information and people than I did when I was young. So that means you can be influenced by an unlimited number of things.

"Influence is the number-one cause of kids doing good or bad. It is imperative that kids be very careful by whom they are influenced. Even though you may not have positive influences in your own home, make a serious effort to find and seek out positive influence somewhere else. Do not succumb to bad influences, no matter what, because in the end, only you will have to pay the price for your wrongdoings. Always try to do what's right. It will pay off in the long run.

"I was influenced by drug dealers. I looked up to them as role models because they had the nice cars, jewelry, homes, etc. Even though I had a good future with my music, instead of putting my focus on my music, I chose to use and sell drugs.

"My drug involvement has cost me twenty-five years of my life in federal prison.

"The smartest thing anyone can do is learn from others' mistakes. I, Ronnie Tape, have set a bad example with my actions as a drug dealer. So I pray that you learn from my mistakes and do good and great things with your life. That's the only good that can come from my situation."

Tape recalled one of his most bittersweet moments prior to his arrest. He flew a friend, Mims Sanders—better known as Daddy Buck and as the father of Deion Sanders—to Los Angeles on a one-way ticket.

"I guess he was just trying to get out of Fort Myers's negative environment," Tape said. "He just had a charisma about him. He really enjoyed himself on that trip. We told him, 'No drugs out here, man.'"

Mims Sanders drank a little alcohol but stayed low-key and enjoyed himself, meeting a few stars like Lionel Richie.

"He was welcome to stay for good, but he said that he would go back to Fort Myers and return later to stay," Tape said.

After returning to Fort Myers, Mims Sanders started using drugs again. The drugs, along with a brain tumor, hastened his death. Tape said he always had a conflicted attitude toward his drug dealing: He enjoyed the money it brought him, but he hated what the drugs did to his friends.

"That broke my heart," Tape said of Mims Sanders dying. "That was sad to see. He was man of such intelligence."

As Tape awaited his freedom, his physical education teacher from so many years ago reflected on the twelve-year-old Tape he once knew.

"I remember Ronnie Tape," said Gerald Copeland, who taught at Fort Myers Middle Academy for thirty-two years and at age seventy was retired and living in Fort Myers. "He was a good boy to me. He did everything I asked him to do. He wanted to be number one. He always tried his best. But you know, he was not a distance runner. He was a sprinter. Whenever I was around, he always listened. He did whatever he could to please me. He never got into any trouble. He always liked to sit down and talk to me. We talked a lot. He sure could shoot the bull. He was one of those kids you could sit down and have a conversation with, and you knew your words weren't going in one ear and out the other."

Copeland said it pained him to learn of the time Tape spent in prison.

"If you hang around with the wrong people, even though you're a pretty good kid, you lose, and you get taken down," Copeland said. "I've seen that time and time again. I've seen some really good athletes have opportunities fall by the wayside. They'd get murdered or go to prison. But then I've seen some really poor people turn around and do some great things, too. So there are some bright spots."

Not long before Tape's downfall, investigators were looking into the possible involvement of Mims Sanders's only son, then a teenaged star athlete. Billie Jones, a member of Tape's drug-dealing enterprise, met with Doug Frazier as part of the investigation of Deion Sanders. Jones would serve five years in prison under a plea-bargain deal for testifying against Tape.

Jones, known as "Uncle Billie," lived in the Left Corner neighborhood. He assured Frazier that Deion Sanders had nothing to do with Ronnie Tape's drug-dealing world. Uncle Billie shielded Deion from the drug trade, which helped Deion avoid at least one of the perils of Dunbar, but not all of them. As a child and young teenager, Deion Sanders had other obstacles with which to contend.

8 Prime's Time

Deion Luwynn Sanders readied himself to race against the speed of light. Darkness had enveloped Dunbar, as Sanders, in middle school during the late 1970s, waited for his chance. As soon as Deion saw approaching headlights, the 70-pound fifth-grader began to sprint. His home, at 1625 Henderson Avenue, sat near the corner of Henderson and Michigan. Across Michigan Avenue rested hundreds of buried bodies at the Fort Myers Cemetery for white people. Across Henderson Avenue and just a few dozen steps from Deion's front door rested the interred bodies at the Oak Ridge Cemetery for blacks. The two cemeteries gave Sanders plenty of reason to run fast at night. They gave him the creeps.

That Deion lived most of his childhood near the corner of where worlds black and white connected made sense, as racial tensions from both sides of the black and white spectrum filled his upbringing.

Born on August 9, 1967, Sanders entered the world in the city of Fort Myers, which had been late to accept integration in schools and in society. To say Sanders isn't the product of a segregated society would be like saying oranges aren't a vital part of Florida's economy. Connie

Mims met Mims Sanders (that her maiden name and his first name were Mims was a coincidence) because of the cultural forces brought on by integration. Connie moved to Fort Myers from Georgia in order to attend classes at Edison Community College, since renamed Florida SouthWestern State College. The school had integrated in 1966–67, the same school year in which Connie enrolled.

Mims Sanders attended Dunbar High School in 1965, but he never graduated. He gained fame there as the flamboyant Dunbar Marching Tigers drum major.

"It was just a handful of us at Edison College during those years," said Dr. Shirley Chapman, who would go on to spend her life as an educator. By "us," she meant African-American students. "We were befriending one another."

Chapman met Connie Mims in one of these small-group settings at the college. Chapman already knew Mims Sanders from Dunbar High School, where everybody knew of the drum major's outgoing personality if they didn't know him personally. "They seemed like a pretty good match," Chapman said. At first, Chapman's hunch proved correct. Mims Sanders and Connie Mims were an instant pair. They entered a life-lasting friendship although not a life-lasting marriage.

"He was so much like Deion," Connie said. "He was cool. He had such an engaging personality. He was so outgoing. We remained friends until he died. He was a wonderful man. He just wasn't cut out for marriage. But he was a loving man."

The Dunbar Marching Tigers, with Mims Sanders guiding them, earned the nickname "Lil FAMU," as they resembled a high school version of the famed Florida A&M marching band. The college band, which drew praise from legions of fans, black and white alike, once visited a Tigers performance. The Florida A&M band witnessed Mims Sanders, who stood in the center of the football field, high-stepping, kneeling, and showboating like nothing anybody in Fort Myers would see again until, a quarter century later, his son Deion Sanders would make similar moves in the end zone.

"He was some kind of drum major," said Chapman, who grew up on Lincoln Boulevard, down the street from the Sanders family. "He was so limber. He could do anything as drum major. And *everybody* was in awe of that. He was really good. And he always had a smile on his face. He was all serious business. You can ask anybody in the Dunbar class of '63, '64, '65, anywhere along then, they will all tell you about Mims Sanders."

And so Connie Mims, a petite, southern black woman from Georgia, arrived in Fort Myers in time to meet Mims Sanders, a local legend. After Deion Sanders rose to fame with the Atlanta Falcons, he introduced his father to rapper MC Hammer and his entourage. Mims Sanders, behind the scenes, toured with Hammer.

Hammer's biggest hit, "Can't Touch This," often applied to Deion as a youth football player. As a fifth-grader, Deion played for a city league team at Shady Oaks Park, a place that in future years would be the field of choice for Noel Devine and other NFL prospects to work out during the summer. In 1976, Noel Devine's father had yet to reach high school, and Deion Sanders turned nine years old.

The streets of Dunbar were chaotic during this era. Unsolved murders happened on a monthly if not weekly basis. Sanders's family insulated him from the dangers around him. Mims Sanders became a drug addict and died in 1993 from a brain tumor. Willie Knight, Sanders's stepfather, was a workaholic and an alcoholic. He died in 1997.

In 1976, both of these men were alive and well. They were, in the words of retired *News-Press* columnist Sam Cook, influencing Sanders like a mixture of oil and water. Mims Sanders did so with his unique form of flamboyancy, his charm, his outgoing personality. Willie Knight did so by demonstrating a work ethic—he labored for thirty years in a lumberyard—that made his stepson feel compelled to give an A-plus effort in all of his endeavors. Their negative influences compelled Connie Knight to find positive influences for her only son.

As Deion reached age nine, his mother saw to it that he received guidance from a coach. She also saw to it that the coach was organized, disciplined, and even that he was white. Although schools were seven years into integration, youth sports teams still were very segregated. That began to change, and it changed under Coach Dave Capel's watch.

"Coach Capel put emphasis on the schoolwork also," Connie Knight said. "Deion had to maintain a certain grade-point average in order to play, and Coach Capel's wife helped the kids with their homework. Coach Capel, he never forgets anything. He remembers everything. I loved him, and I love him to this day."

"Deion was on the Jets team," Dave Capel said of the first time he saw Deion Sanders. Capel coached the Cowboys before coaching Deion with the Rebels. He died at age seventy-seven in August 2011. Fortunately, I had the opportunity to spend time with him before he died. More than just an interview subject, he became a friend.

"Whenever we played against them at Shady Oaks, they couldn't catch us," Capel told me. "We ran the wishbone. We whipped them real good. I think we beat them 48–7. They couldn't compete against us."

After the game, Connie Knight approached Capel about having her son switch teams the following season. She had a deeper reasoning than wanting her son on a powerhouse. She recognized that Capel ran his teams with more precision and more discipline than the teams from her neighborhood. Capel, who had a day job selling and installing window blinds and draperies, had a growing reputation as a youth football coach as well. He was known as someone who stressed to youngsters the value of working hard in school. Years later, Capel carried the proof to back it up. His wife, Helen, tracked and kept the grade-point averages of each of his players as well as the cumulative grade-point average for each of his youth football teams.

"When we got Deion, he was a B-minus student," Capel said, as his eyes began to smile. "When he left, he was a B-plus student."

When Capel accepted Sanders on his Pop Warner team in 1977, the organization called itself the Rebels, an ode to Lee County's namesake, confederate general Robert E. Lee. All five assistant coaches on Capel's staff were white, and they reserved spots for only a handful of black players. That first season, Capel picked only three black players: one for offense (Deion), one for defense, and one for special teams. The white coaches thought that having too many black players would cause team dissension because the black players all wanted the ball, and they all wanted to dominate the skill positions of running back and wide receiver. Get a handful of black athletes, spread them into different facets of the team, and the team would thrive, Capel figured. In 1977, most of the black athletes played for the Tice Tigers youth football organization. The white players and the tiniest fraction of black players, including Deion, made up the Rebels.

Sanders was the only black child on his Little League baseball team as well.

"I was the Jackie Robinson of my Little League team," Sanders said.

Like Robinson, Sanders had to suffer for being a pioneer. He had to deal with criticisms from both sides of the racial divide.

"You got ridiculed," Sanders said of his black peers and their coaches. "First of all, when I played with the Rebels, they'd say, 'You're playing with all them white boys!' The biggest matchup came when we played against Dunbar. So when the time came, they wanted me to cross the Jordan River."

Sanders did not enjoy the ribbing, but he did not regret the experience either. He credited his mother with finding a positive environment for him as a youth athlete.

"She always sacrificed in looking out for me," Sanders said. "She wanted to see me in things that were structured. Things that were healthy. Wholesome. But there was not a lot of structure over there. They were not very organized."

Sanders never had more than four black teammates during his three seasons under Capel with the Rebels. This gave Sanders more exposure to white culture and society than most of his peers in Dunbar.

During the late 1970s, just prior to starting his teenage years, Sanders found his first vision of success. The perfect picture of his future entered his mind when he first saw the long driveway of Pop Warner football teammate Billy Johnson.

Billy Johnson lived off McGregor Boulevard, next door to the Thomas Edison and Henry Ford estates. The five-bedroom, four-bathroom house sat a stone's throw from the Caloosahatchee River.

"It was a vision," Sanders told me in January 2011, during my interview with him for the *News-Press*. "It was a vision of seeing Billy Johnson's house. I'd go over to his house. He had a swimming pool and a tennis court. He befriended me. I was an African-American kid, and he and his family befriended me. They treated me like family. His mother was unbelievable. His father was a dentist. When I went to the pros, there was something to me about a long driveway. I always said to myself, 'The longer your driveway is, the better your money is.'"

Sanders has quite a long driveway. He built his ten-bedroom, 39,000-square-foot home in Prosper on a 100-acre lot. To compare, another Fort Myers icon, inventor Thomas Edison, had his own grand home built off McGregor Boulevard—on 14 acres. Edison's home had an outdoor pool but not an indoor one like Deion's. It had a botanical garden, but it did not have a full-size football field in the backyard. Nor did it have a driveway measuring at least a quarter mile long.

While the driveway in front of Billy Johnson's house always stuck in the back of Sanders's mind, excelling in sports remained at the front of it. Sanders won his first national championship as a Pop Warner player for Coach Capel's Rebels. A few years later, during a team meeting at Florida State prior to playing a big game, Coach Bobby Bowden gathered his players together for a pep talk.

"How many of you have ever won a national championship?" Bowden asked them, figuring none of them would raise their hands. Deion raised his hand.

"I did, Coach!" Sanders said, practically spoiling Bowden's purpose of the pep talk. "My team won the Pop Warner national title!"

For three seasons, in 1977–79, Capel deployed Deion, ages ten to twelve, as a running back on the Fort Myers Rebels Dynomites. The Dynomites dominated their opponents, finishing with 12–1, 13–0, and 13–0 records. Entering 1979, Capel learned his team would be recognized by the Pop Warner organization as the national champion if it went undefeated while maintaining an A–B grade point average, which it did. While Deion continued to improve as a student, he continued to perform on the field as well, and to a level Capel never had seen from any other child.

"Misdirections, reverses, crisscrosses," Capel said of the strategies when deploying Deion. "Getting him one-on-one, that's how we succeeded."

This wasn't the six-foot, one-inch, 190-pound Sanders playing for the San Francisco 49ers and winning his first Super Bowl, which he did during the 1994 NFL season. This was a 70-pound ten-year-old whose team finished ranked sixteenth in the nation. This was a 77-pound eleven-year-old whose team finished ranked fourth in the nation. This was an 88-pound twelve-year-old who helped guide his thirty-five-player team and the nineteen Dynomite cheerleaders to the 1979 Pop Warner national championship game. The Dynomites defeated the DeKalb County, Georgia, Chargers 26–0. Deion and his teammates appeared the following season on the cover of Pop Warner football's sign-up brochure. It marked the first of many times Sanders would be on the cover of a national publication. Capel had the foresight to keep the brochure. Capel seemed to keep everything, including a copy of the February 29, 1980, announcement in which Fort Myers mayor Burl A. Underhill signed a proclamation declaring March 2, 1980, as Fort Myers Rebel Dynomite Day.

All the while, the streets of Fort Myers continued to deteriorate into a drug-infested swamp covered by concrete. In playing Pop Warner football, Deion avoided running the streets of his hometown. Mims Sanders spiraled into a two-decade-long battle with substance abuse. He could get away with it among his friends because of his jovial personality, but he could not appease his wife.

After Mims Sanders and Connie divorced, she and Deion lived in the Jones Walker Apartment Complex on Blount Street, an eighty-unit property that seemed to deteriorate with each passing year because of drugs and crime. Eventually, Connie met Willie Knight and fell in love. They married and moved to 1625 Henderson, a modest, two-bedroom, one-bathroom home across the street from the cemeteries.

Throughout high school, Sanders dealt with the repercussions of living in one of the most segregated cities of the South. Being bused across the river to a white school instead of staying at home, where Dunbar High had closed for integration, bothered him into adulthood, as it did many other black students from Fort Myers. Why couldn't the white students have been bused to the black school? Why didn't the white politicians allow the black men and women to keep the pillar of their community intact, their high school?

Dunbar High eventually reopened in 2000, and the court order for desegregated schools expired in 2003. In 2014, Dunbar High underwent a $35 million renovation, a project that came thirty years too late for Sanders's taste.

"You were at North Fort Myers, man," Sanders said of the school situation. "They were busing you over there. Think about it. You were living on Henderson Avenue, and you were bused to North Fort Myers. Why wasn't there a high school in our neighborhood to facilitate us? Think about it. You're living on the other side of the city, and you're bused almost all the way to Cape Coral."

Some of the black children never had been out of Dunbar, Sanders said. They never had crossed the river.

"Think about it," Sanders said.

At North Fort Myers High, Sanders saw racism from the other spectrum. A few of the low-income white students—the "rednecks"—sometimes threatened Sanders, especially when he began dating a white girl. At one point, Sanders carried a baseball bat with him for protection. He also carried it because he played baseball. He also excelled at basketball and, of course, football, playing at an All-American level in all three sports.

"You know what my biggest play was?" Sanders said. "I was walking through campus, and there was this fight. I saw this one kid, larger than the other kid, getting the best of him. I pulled the kid off the other kid, and I found out his name was Bert Cool. I broke up that fight, and I told that little man, 'If you ever need anything, let me know.' Me and the kid was cool. Bert Cool. That was probably my biggest play. Helping out kids, man. Helping out kids."

By the mid-1980s, when Sanders reached high school, the white coaches were well past the notion of fielding as few black players as possible. North coach Ron Hoover wore tube socks pulled up to his knees, a pair of red Bike-brand shorts that he pulled up over his navel, Riddell-brand coaching shoes, and a silver whistle around his neck. He usually stuffed a brown clipboard holding plays and practice plans into his shorts. He allowed the best players to play, and he benched anyone with discipline problems.

"He was old-school, man," Sanders said.

Hoover had grown up in tiny Appleton City, Missouri, just south of Kansas City, in what he described as a "country town" of about two thousand people. Born on September 14, 1933, Hoover lived in Arizona in the mid-1940s. His father worked on the railroad as a brakeman.

After his parents divorced, he moved back to Missouri. In 1951, at the age of eighteen, he enlisted in the Navy and was stationed in Honolulu during the Korean War. In 1959, he made his way to Fort Myers as a physical education and social studies teacher, landing at Lee Middle School, later renamed after James Stephens. In 1968, he ended up at North Fort Myers High, just before school desegregation began.

"When we broke up Dunbar, it was like a pie," Hoover said. "We got so many players. Cypress Lake High School got so many, and Fort Myers High School got so many. We all got a piece of the pie."

In 1982, Hoover landed a big piece of the pie in getting Deion Sanders. Hoover had been watching Deion rise through the ranks of Pop Warner football.

"I remember the first time I saw him. He was all-everything in Pop Warner. Deion's legs were about that big around," Hoover said, shaping one hand into a small circle. "I said, 'He might be a good basketball player, but he's awfully little to be playing football.'"

By 1983, Hoover had no choice but to change his assessment of Sanders, starting him at quarterback. Sanders, who wore uniform number 29 with the Dynomites, wore number 10 with the Red Knights.

"Let me tell you who Ron Hoover was," Sanders said. "First of all, Ron Hoover stood for discipline. He stood for what was right. He stood for hard work, determination, and focus."

Some of the black athletes at North High quit the team because they couldn't take Hoover's heat.

"I was amazed," Sanders said. "A lot of the best players didn't even play football because they didn't want to adhere to Coach Hoover, who wanted to be the best. He loved kids. He wanted to see you to the next level. He had a team rule that if you got suspended, you got kicked off the team. And I got suspended—even though to this day, it wasn't my fault.

"I was in the library, talking to somebody, and this teacher came up to me really rude. She told me I was being insubordinate. Nevertheless, I ended up getting suspended and kicked off the team.

"But nevertheless, that was really profound. I needed it. It lets you know, you aren't any better than anyone else. You must abide by the rules like everybody else, no matter who you are, no matter what position you played. And I came back my senior year with a whole new attitude. I was much more respectful of adults. I was much more understanding of the position of being a leader. And I had much more respect for Coach Hoover. He could have said, 'Oh, I'll waive my rule for him.' And he didn't do that."

Years later, Hoover still did not like to talk about having to kick Sanders off his football team.

"I feel bad, because I was probably the only coach who ever fired Deion," Hoover said. He's wrong, though; the Dallas Cowboys released Sanders in a cost-cutting move after 1999.

Hoover is correct, however, in his assessment that this incident further shaped Sanders.

"His senior year, he was everything you wanted in a player," Hoover said. "He was my hardest worker. He did everything you wanted him to do. He wanted to be the best, and he was the best."

While many of the athletes and friends around him sold and did drugs, Sanders never did. He insisted that he never even tried a sip of alcohol, never took a drag of a cigarette, never took a hit of marijuana. He never took his focus off the task at hand, which was becoming the best athlete he could be and, later in life, becoming the best coach of youth athletes he could possibly be.

Sanders blossomed as an athlete at Florida State University. He chose the Seminoles over the Georgia Bulldogs and Florida Gators for reasons that had less to do with the mystique of Doak Campbell Stadium and legendary coach Bobby Bowden and more to do with something else he learned on his recruiting visits. Coming from Dunbar, where Sanders had to endure economic hardships, racial injustice, and constant pressure to perform as an athlete and to conform in the neighborhood, Sanders also taught a lesson to those who courted him: Never slight Deion Sanders.

"I went to the University of Georgia," Sanders said of his first recruiting trip. "Vince Dooley is the head coach. I had just witnessed them getting their butts kicked against Georgia Tech. I went into Vince Dooley's office. And he says, 'Well, I'm sure you're going to contribute for us. I want you to redshirt and learn the system.'

"And I said, 'Redshirt?'

"And that was it. He's talking about redshirting, and I know what I've got. So that was it. I crossed him off the list."

Next up: the University of Florida in Gainesville.

"In the locker, they put your numbers on the back of the recruits' jerseys. There was another kid with the same number I had. They had a jersey made up with number 10. And they had another one made up with number 10. You can't have two number 10s. That was a mistake. Cross them off the list."

Finally, Sanders visited Florida State in Tallahassee.

"Everything was wonderful," Sanders said. "But the best thing they did was in the cafeteria. They had a lady named Miss Betty. Miss Betty, African-American lady. The cafeteria was like the Golden Corral, which is one of my favorite restaurants. I knew I couldn't cook. I couldn't even warm up anything, because my mama did everything. She always made food, or my stepdaddy did."

Miss Betty's home-style cooking in the FSU cafeteria brought Sanders to the right place at the right time. Coach Bowden, who would finish his coaching career with thirty-four years of tenure at Florida State, also sealed the deal.

"Coach Bowden and [defensive coordinator] Mickey Andrews never talked about redshirting or anything," Sanders said. "He talked about, 'You're going to be educated, and you're going to have a chance to play like everybody else. And that's the deal.' And that was all I wanted. It was a done deal. Florida State was wonderful, man. It was wonderful."

Sanders would go on to intercept 14 passes in his college career and be named All-American in 1987 and 1988. He returned one of his interceptions 100 yards for a score. He led the nation in punt return average in 1988 and had his jersey number 2 retired in 1995.

"He's the best athlete I've ever coached," Bowden said more than twenty-five years later when we crossed paths at a Fellowship of Christian Athletes meeting. "It isn't even close, just on athletic ability alone. I might have had some who were more valuable. Charlie Ward might have been more valuable. Warrick Dunn might have been more valuable. But none of them were as good of a player as Deion."

As a senior in college, Sanders signed with the New York Yankees and positioned himself to become a two-sport professional sports superstar. The top baseball franchise in the land had secured his services, so Sanders needed a home for his football talents. Although the NFL has a draft, Sanders pretty much dictated where he would land.

"I didn't want to go nowhere but Atlanta," Sanders said.

The reasons were many, and they stemmed from his childhood experiences in Dunbar. In Atlanta, Sanders saw a city full of success stories for African Americans. He saw a city where he belonged, a city where he could thrive.

"It's because they could understand me," Sanders said. "I believed in it. I went to Atlanta one time, and I can remember seeing all of these African Americans running businesses. I had never seen that before, coming from Fort Myers. I had never seen it before. It amazed me, man. I liked how I could carry myself there. So that was where I wanted to go.

"We drafted each other. I let everybody know, I would not play anywhere but there."

Unlike nearly all other NFL prospects before or since, Sanders had the leverage to get away with such demands. He already had a professional sports contract in hand, courtesy of the Yankees, who took him in the thirtieth round of the 1988 draft. Sanders said his "welcome to the NFL moment" happened not in a game but between games.

"Well, I got there on a Thursday, and I played that Sunday," Sanders said of his debut with the Falcons. He scored in his first game. "I had hit a home run that week, too. That was normalcy for me. But once I did that, I was getting calls from everywhere. 'They want you on *Monday Night Football*. They want you to do this. They want you to do that.' And I was like, 'For what? I've been doing this since I was a kid.'

"That's when I realized, you're in the pros now. I never sat back and said, 'Man, I can't believe I did that.' That was just what I did. It was what I did ever since I was a kid. So that was probably my moment, realizing I was in the pros now."

Sanders also recognized an entry point to superstardom. Former NFL defensive back Richard Fain, a high school teammate of Sanders at North Fort Myers High School, bestowed the "Prime Time" nickname upon him during their 1983–84 basketball season because they played their games during TV prime time. Soon, Sanders took his nickname national.

"I went to Florida State with Prime Time on my license plate," Sanders said. "Then it became just an understanding of the nature of the business. Defensive backs were being paid like offensive lineman. So I perpetuated the persona, because I knew it would be something that people would notice. I knew I had to take it to another level. But sometimes, people didn't understand the method to all the madness. Sort of like the jewelry."

The jewelry—the chains, the rings, the earrings, the silver, the gold, the platinum—had its roots in Dunbar, too.

"All the kids in Fort Myers, who did they have to look up to at that time?" Sanders said. "They looked up to the drug dealers. They had the girls, they had the cars, they had all of that. I wanted to show the kids, 'I'm going to do things the right way. I'm not going to do it through drugs. I'm going to do it the right way.'"

Sanders did things his own way. His methods were good enough for enshrinement in the Pro Football Hall of Fame. Upon the announcement of his election, Sanders did not wear a coat and tie like his freshly elected peers. Nor did he sit with them in the NFL Network studio at the 2011 Super Bowl media center in Dallas. Instead, Sanders wore cleats and stood on a mud-caked youth football field in Lancaster, Texas, about twenty-six miles south of where hundreds of reporters waited for him. A black whistle hung around his neck. He wore a black hooded sweatshirt, embroidered in red with one word on it: Truth.

Just after 6:30 p.m. CST on Saturday, February 5, 2011, the eve of Super Bowl Sunday, Sanders had just finished coaching thirteen-, fourteen-, and fifteen-year-old children. They were on the losing end of a 57–12 score against rapper Snoop Dogg's team from Los Angeles.

Snoop Dogg fielded the call from an NFL official who relayed the news.

"I would like to say," Snoop Dogg said through a miniature microphone, "will somebody please welcome Deion Sanders to the 2011 NFL Hall of Fame!"

Applause engulfed the youth football field, where hundreds of parents, players, and fans had gathered, representing five states and six youth football programs for what was dubbed the "Snoop Bowl." They had braved a frosty morning and gotten off to a late start, clearing a park that resembled a hockey rink more than a football field, thanks to the remnants of an ice storm that hit North Texas during Super Bowl week. Sanders never wavered and never considered canceling this event, even after part of his mansion's roof caved in after a frozen pipe burst. Everything unfolded in this moment almost exactly as Sanders had foreseen.

"You've got to kiss the wife," Snoop Dogg said as Sanders approached his then-wife Pilar Sanders, with an NFL Network film crew capturing the scene.

"Kiss the wife," Snoop Dogg kept saying. "There you go, Prime. There you go, Prime."

Sanders then hugged and kissed his oldest son, Deion Sanders Jr.; his younger sons, Shilo and Shedeur; his daughter, Shelomi; his mother, Connie Knight; and his sister, Tracie Knight.

"Can we have a moment of prayer real quick?" Snoop Dogg beckoned them. "Bow your heads real quick."

For the first time as an elected member of the Pro Football Hall of Fame, Sanders clasped his hands together and prayed.

"I want to thank You for filling us with this great atmosphere," Snoop Dogg said. "Thank You for putting Deion Sanders on this earth to give us something to look up to. God bless you, Prime Time.

"Amen."

And then, as the youth football games continued, dark-suited men wearing sunglasses and earpieces and resembling Secret Service agents whisked Sanders and most of his immediate family away. They turned a marathon drive into a sprint, high-tailing it to the Sheraton in downtown Dallas, which had been transformed into the Super Bowl media center. There, the NFL Network set awaited Sanders. Newly elected Hall-of-Famers tight end Shannon Sharpe and running back Marshall Faulk already were onstage. Unlike Sanders, who still wore his sweatpants and hooded sweatshirt, they were wearing thousand-dollar suits.

Sanders joined Sharpe and Faulk as perhaps two hundred sportswriters from across the country and even a few dozen from around the world convened. NFL Network extended its broadcast an extra hour in order to accommodate Sanders's whirlwind schedule of coaching a half dozen youth football games. After a video of highlights from Sanders's career, Sanders spoke.

"Next to the Bible, my favorite book was *The Little Engine That Could*," Sanders said. "I read that story so many times, I know it by heart. And a couple of trains passed that engine until he started saying to himself, 'I think I can. I think I can. I think I can.' And that's what I modeled my career after. I mean, it sounds arrogant. It sounds brash. It sounds cocky. But it was real."

The only athlete to play in a World Series and a Super Bowl, Sanders finished his professional football career with 22 touchdowns, 9 of which were on interception returns. Sanders played for five teams during fourteen seasons, 1989–2000 and 2004–5. The fifth overall pick in the 1989 NFL Draft by the Atlanta Falcons, he won back-to-back Super Bowl rings in capping the 1994–95 seasons, one with the San Francisco 49ers and another with the Dallas Cowboys. His legend grew. He released a rap CD ("Must Be the Money" was the marketed single), published a book (*Power, Money & Sex: How Success Almost Ruined My Life*), hosted *Saturday Night Live* (on February 18, 1995, less than a month after winning his first Super Bowl), and appeared on the October 9, 1995, cover of *Sports Illustrated* wearing a fresh, white, Dallas Cowboys number 21 jersey (the headline: "Why Is This Man Worth $35 Million?").

A standout base runner and base stealer, Sanders also played nine seasons in professional baseball, taking the field in the majors for the Yankees, Braves, Reds, and Giants.

The career accolades and Pro Football Hall of Fame election and induction could not have happened without his humble roots and his devotion to his mother, Connie Knight.

"She worked at Lee Memorial Hospital in Fort Myers, Florida," Sanders said. Sometimes he lied to his friends, telling them that she worked as a nurse instead of on the cleaning staff. "I told my mom that someday, I'm going to be rich, and you're never going to have to work a day for the rest of your life. So that was my promise."

. . . .

Calvin Church, who lived in the Sabal Palm apartment projects as a child, never reached the NFL as Sanders did, but he crossed paths with many others who did. Church played football at Riverdale High School for three seasons, 1976–78, before transferring to Cape Coral High and graduating from there in 1980. Over the years that followed, he coached or saw most of Dunbar's future NFL players when they were in youth football. His son is a cousin of Deion Sanders.

"Deion's dad was my flag football coach," Church said of Mims Sanders. "He was fresh out of high school. The high-step and carrying the ball with two hands? Deion got that from me. We'd carry the ball with two hands, getting ready to pitch it. Deion saw that as a young kid. The celebrating and all that stuff? He saw us doing that."

Church said he had twenty-three Division I scholarship offers coming out of high school. His youngest brother, Johnie Church, graduated from Cypress Lake, played defensive end for the Florida Gators, and became a seventh-round NFL Draft pick by the Seattle Seahawks in 1996, only to be released. Johnie Church tore his hamstring while with the Jacksonville Jaguars in 1997 and never got to play in the NFL.

While Johnie Church suffered an injury, Calvin Church had a different obstacle in his path, not just to the NFL but to Division I college football. He did not know how to read. To this day, Calvin Church cannot read.

"When I got to high school, my freshman year at Riverdale, I played running back, wide receiver, safety and corner," Calvin Church said. "My sophomore year, they started putting me at nose guard. When they snapped the ball, I'd already be in the backfield, tackling people."

Church weighed 175 pounds and said he ran the 40-yard dash in 4.2 seconds.

"The city was so small then," he said of the 1970s and 1980s. "A lot of kids got shoved under the bus. The bigger the city grew, the more the city helped these kids and guided them the right way. Back in '82, we had a ton of talent on our flag football team. We went around the state of Florida, playing other teams in flag football. Every team that we played had former NFL players or Division I players on their flag football team. We'd still go out there and beat them. That let me know right then the caliber of football in Fort Myers was too good.

"It's just that the kids in Fort Myers didn't have the role model and solid parenting. The streets would gobble them up right quick. There was so much going on, back in '85 and '86 with the streets. All of it came down to the drugs."

Drug dealing appealed to Dunbar teenagers and young adults because it allowed them to escape poverty fast. All of the socioeconomic forces that led the black youth of Fort Myers astray into the drug trade, Church said, stemmed from slavery a century earlier.

"The jobs are limited for minorities, even the ones with college degrees," Church said. "A lot of them would move up North to where they could get jobs. It was still so backwards. It's so hard for a minority, with a degree, to get a job. There are no opportunities for athletes to come back and help the city."

The lack of job opportunities for college-educated blacks in Fort Myers led to many of them leaving the city to pursue careers. That migration meant the youth left behind had very few black businessmen and role models around them. Youngsters such as Jevon Kearse and Jammi German grew up focused on one thing: getting good in football so they could get out of town.

"It has changed a lot," Church said of Dunbar. "It's much scarier now. A lot of guys are running around, and they have no direction. If you're a kid already on the wrong road, they don't care about you. Back in the day, when Jammi German was coming up, when they caught him doing wrong, they'd chase him away."

Jammi's Journey

Two teenagers barged into Jammi German's home at 8613 Willard Street in what was known as the New Projects. One of them lived next door. Just seconds earlier, fourteen-year-old German had heard the gunshots that killed two neighbors. Then the two teenagers—one the triggerman, the other an accomplice—arrived seeking sanctuary.

They were not fighting over gang turf or a girl. They were arguing over a stolen, homemade hood ornament from a car.

"My mom told him he needed to turn himself in to the police," German said years later. He paused, reliving the incident while sitting in the comfort of his south Fort Myers condominium, safe within a gated community.

"I guess the moral of the story is, we were probably the only ones who made it out of the projects to go on to college," German said of himself, older brother Melvin German Jr., and their siblings. "Most of the kids who grew up in my neighborhood are either dead, in prison, or did prison time or something like that. I'd say it was about four in a hundred who made it out of the New Projects."

Born on the Fourth of July in 1974, Jammi German lived in a two-parent household through age fourteen. His family stood out because his parents, Melvin German Sr. and Clare, had stayed together for so long. That aspect of German's childhood played a crucial role in German avoiding the fate of so many of his childhood friends in Dunbar.

"I had my dad in the house, almost all the way up," German said. "Very few families have that." Having a stable, two-parent household provided German a discipline most of his friends and neighbors lacked. Clare German worked at the Edison Mall's Sears department store. Melvin German Sr. worked construction by day and sang for a rhythm-and-blues band by night. He would come home from long, hard days, and he had a level of expectation for his children. They had chores. Everybody had something to do. Even though they lived in the projects, their house wasn't the projects. That's what Clare German liked to say. When the time arrived to go to bed, the dishes were clean and put away, and neither Clare nor Melvin German Sr. had lifted a finger.

In the early years, the German family enjoyed better lives than their neighbors. They eventually moved out of the New Projects, away from Dunbar, and into another low-income neighborhood.

"We felt like we were further up," Jammi German said. "We actually had a pool at our place. We lived there about three years. And then we ended up moving again."

About the same time that *Miami Vice* hit the television airwaves, something else was in the air during the mid- to late 1980s, when Jammi German headed toward his destiny of becoming the most decorated high school football player in Lee County history. German became the inaugural Florida Mr. Football award winner, a Parade All-American, a selection to the Florida-Georgia All-Star Game, and finally, the *USA Today* Defensive Player of the Year in 1992.

Before all of that, German was just trying to survive the fallout from his parents' fractured love and the lure of the street scene in Dunbar, where he learned fast to forsake trying crack cocaine despite selling it while in middle school.

"That's when the crack rock came out," Jammi German said. "That's when a lot of the crime took off. Once the crack rock hit, the projects went crazy. I saw family members do drugs. Selling drugs. That's why we moved out of the projects." As tough as his life had been in the projects, it got even tougher after they moved out.

"When my mom and dad were together, we had a beautiful household," German said. "When my dad was in the household, I was more conscious of my wrongs and rights. When you don't have a dad in the home, it makes it a lot tougher."

By 1985, Melvin German Sr. had spiraled into a crack cocaine addiction that splintered the family and almost ended his life. Born on March 11, 1951, Melvin German Sr. grew up in Philadelphia. He moved to Tampa as a teenager, attending the then-segregated Middleton High School before dropping out in eleventh grade. He became the lead singer of a six-piece rhythm-and-blues band called Sag War Fare. The band took its name as a variation of "Savoir-Faire," the name of the cartoon mouse from the 1960s TV series *Klondike Kat*, one of Melvin German's favorite shows. In French, having *savoir faire* means being adaptable and adroit, able to adapt to any situation.

In 1971, the band's bass player insisted on playing a gig at the Dixon Bar off Anderson Avenue in Fort Myers. Melvin met Clare soon thereafter, and he never left town. Not long after Melvin settled in Fort Myers, temptation—in the form of heroin—claimed the trumpet player. Melvin German waited for his turn to shoot up after a show. Smoke filled the room, and heroin filled a bowl. The trumpet player injected himself with the needle. German saw the look of what appeared to be agony, not ecstasy, on his friend's face and bolted from the room.

"Bam!" German said. "I got out of that house fast. I never did that. Nuh-uh. Never."

Making a name for himself as a musician, Melvin German Sr. also made himself a man to be respected by winning a street brawl. He knocked out his opponent after a knock-down, drag-out fight, one typical of the 1970s in Dunbar.

"Back then, that's how they settled things," said Jammi German, who did not witness the fight but learned of its legend years later. "Nowadays, they just shoot each other and everything else."

While Melvin German Sr. had gained respect as a member of the community, he lost his self-respect for a time by becoming addicted to crack cocaine. It all happened so fast at Club 82, off Anderson Avenue.

German and the band were on stage playing, and a bandmate had the crack onstage. He smoked some.

"The first hit—addicted," Melvin German Sr. said. "When I did it, I thought I was on cloud nine. That stuff is that potent. Everybody is walking around, and you want more. You want more. You want more."

Subsequent uses of crack, which cost ten dollars a rock, never resulted in the ecstasy of that first high, German said. He shifted his dedication from his wife and his family to trying to find the pleasure of that first hit and high of crack cocaine. By that time, Dunbar had earned the nickname "Cracktown, U.S.A." in national law enforcement circles.

"I kept doing it and doing it and doing it until it destroyed my family," Melvin German Sr. said. "Crack was the worst drug ever in the United States. It ain't hard to get started on that stuff. If you try it, I'm telling you, you'll get addicted to it that first hit. And it will destroy you and your family."

Six or seven years after being strung out on crack, German eventually overcame the addiction. He did so in large part by praying about it. Losing his family planted the seeds for him to quit. He never could repair the damage inflicted upon his marriage. The divorce would have lasting repercussions for Jammi German, a teenager when his parents separated.

The divorce factored into Jammi German being there for his own son later in his life. German spent his post-NFL days working for the Lee County School District and being an involved father to his son. "I don't want to be a statistic," German said. "I don't want my son to have a stepdad. We've got to bridge the gap.

"Once my mom and dad separated, I went nuts. I got into the streets. I got into doing all the bad things."

Jammi German didn't play much youth football, although he followed the NFL.

"Deion went to the league and tore it up," German said. "I had posters of Deion all throughout the house. Michael Jordan and Deion, those were my posters. Prime Time was everything to me as an athlete. And he could walk the talk, too. I loved his interviews."

Once his parents separated, German found himself and his family, minus his father, living on the eastern edge of Dunbar near Billy Bow-legs Park, where Sanders once played Little League baseball. The neighborhoods around the park had transformed into yet another haven for hiding and dealing drugs.

"I was nickel and diming," German said of his brief foray into small-time drug dealing. "We moved into where the biggest dope dealers were. We saw stuff go down. I'm talking about garbage cans full of dope or full of money. It used to go down. That's when the phenomenon was in full swing. I would find anything and everything to get into. I was rebellious. We're in the neighborhood and look what I see, but without the disciplinarian in the house."

The big dealers lived in the neighborhood and would start with a "pack," which consisted of one hundred pieces of crack cocaine. As that dealer distributed to other smaller dealers, including Jammi German, the pack would be splintered into fragments, with each successive dealer receiving less and less of the product while charging more for it. This continued to go down in 1989, when German went to Riverdale High School in east Fort Myers as a freshman. He and his older brother Melvin Jr. then got expelled from Riverdale for fighting. They were sent to the Alternative Learning Center (ALC) off Michigan Avenue, just down the street from Sanders's childhood home. German described the fight as a "riot," with one clique of young black friends taking on another. He could not recall the reason for the fight, but it played a huge part in setting him and Melvin Jr. on a better path. The German brothers first had to endure the ALC, a school for the worst-behaved of the worst-behaved. These were the students expelled from the other Lee County high schools. One fellow student brought crack to campus and sold it for twenty to thirty dollars. Jammi said he bought and resold some of that student's drugs. He said he never tried crack. Seeing what it did to his father and other family members scared him.

"I wasn't good at it, being on the corner, trying to sell crack," Jammi German said. "I tried that for a couple of months." German did so more out of boredom than for money. He felt like he did not belong at the ALC. Years later, German would end up working there as a security guard. Over the course of a few years, German learned how to spot students who were part of gangs, sold drugs, were looking for trouble, or all of the above. When fights broke out on campus, German would be in the middle of them, breaking them up.

"We were smart kids," German said, recalling his and his brother's time as students there. "ALC was so slow, we thought the other kids were dumb. We had to stay there for forty-five days. But we couldn't go back to Riverdale."

Melvin and Jammi ended up at Fort Myers High School, a move that changed their lives for the better. Before the first day of school, then–Fort Myers principal Herbert Wiseman and another school official met with the German brothers and their mother. The two men let the Germans know that Fort Myers had established itself as a prestigious school. They knew of the boys' transgressions at Riverdale and at the ALC and announced that they would not be putting up with any such behavior.

The Germans were not afforded any favors. Jammi German had not played youth football since ages ten and eleven. In the fall of 1990, Melvin, a senior, and Jammi, a sophmore, opted to try out for the Fort Myers football team. On the first day of practice, Jammi almost left, intending to buy a bottle of malt liquor with a brown paper bag at a Dunbar corner store that sold alcohol to minors. Melvin urged his brother to stay at practice. As usual, Jammi listened to his older brother. He did so in the classroom, too. When Melvin started doing his homework, so did Jammi.

The late Fort Myers High School coach Sam Sirianni Sr., on his way to local legendary status and a thirty-three-year career guiding the Green Wave, instructed the Germans to start on the junior varsity team. That stint lasted all of a few minutes. Just before practice began, Jammi, standing outside Edison Stadium, did a standing leap over the chain-link fence and landed on the track.

"You all move your stuff down to varsity," Sirianni told them. He immediately started Melvin at strong safety and put Jammi at free safety.

Jammi German suddenly was receiving daily doses of discipline again, this time from Sirianni. "My dad gave him a structure," said Sam Sirianni Jr., who succeeded his father as coach after he died from a rare form of bladder cancer in October 2002. "When Jammi's family split, he got to be a wild stallion and got into trouble. He was looking for a male figure to be firm with him and somebody he could trust with his best interests. They had a good relationship from right away. Jammi was never a problem for us."

Jammi wore uniform number 15 in his sophomore season. He picked off 7 passes, one of which he returned 85 yards for a touchdown. The Green Wave went 9–1.

"When I was number 15, that's when I was known for knocking people out," Jammi said. He considered his high school sophomore season one of the best experiences of his life because he played alongside his brother. "That was the best football ever," Jammi said. "Better than the NFL. Better than Miami. Better than everything. I'd get an interception, he would run up to me and say, 'I got the next one.' In the middle of the game, he would say this. Then he would go out and do it."

Sam Sirianni Jr., German's offensive coordinator that season, called German the best college recruit ever to come out of Fort Myers. No offense to Deion Sanders before him or Earnest Graham, Noel Devine, or Sammy Watkins after him, but Jammi German was the 1992 *USA Today* Defensive Player of the Year.

"It didn't take long to know he had talent," Sirianni Jr. said of German. "It didn't take five minutes to realize there was special ability there. Even though he didn't play a lot of youth football, he had a keen IQ for the game. He took to learning very easily. He could play within the scheme of what you were doing. You had to tame the stallion a little bit. He had such a motor. As he was learning the game, we had to hold him back a little bit.

"That was the thing about Jammi. When he got to our school, coming off the trouble, we wondered if he would fit in. For all of his ability, is it going to be a tug-of-war? Would he be a good part of the team? That was never an issue. From the first thing he did, he went 100 miles an hour. It was like the weight of the world was off his shoulders, getting a fresh start. Jammi practiced like he played. There were no days off. He never saved himself for Friday. He sent a message to everybody because everything he did was 100 percent.

"Nobody really wanted Jammi German because of the baggage he had. For whatever reason and maybe the change of environment, he grew up. He became what he became."

German would have been a YouTube phenomenom. As a sophomore, German delivered bone-crushing hits. As a junior, German joined the offense as an integral piece. Then he started returning kicks. The Green Wave went 10–3 and lost in the state semifinals to undefeated St. Thomas Aquinas of Fort Lauderdale. German finished that season with 18 catches for 466 yards, scoring 13 touchdowns and landing on the All-State first team. He realized for the first time heading into his junior season that football could take him someplace. Teammates Rod Gadson, a future Syracuse University cornerback, and Keith "Feed the World" Drayton, a future defensive tackle at Georgia, also were drawing college recruiters to campus.

"That's when we realized that everybody could go to school," German said. "I passed the SAT my junior year."

As a senior, German did it all. The starting fullback, Clifton Green, blew out his knee early in the season. Jammi German played tailback at times. Fort Myers went 12–1, falling again to St. Thomas Aquinas 28–0. German finished the season with 16 catches for 456 yards, scoring 11 touchdowns despite playing most of the season with an ankle injury. The Siriannis began limiting German's carries, trying to preserve him for the playoffs.

"If you let him touch the ball twenty times, he was going to break three or four," Sirianni Jr. said. "If there's ever one what-if as a coach, if we had him healthy against Aquinas, I believe, I know it would have been a different game. We played him at wideout. He played, but he wasn't the same Jammi from before the injury."

Jammi relished the local and national spotlights during his senior year. Flashing his six gold teeth, ones he would replace with white ones midway through college, Jammi smiled on the cover of the *News-Press* high school football preview section, the theme of which centered on his dream of playing Division I college football. It had a bubble cloud of college choices above Jammi's head. Miami, Syracuse, and Florida were his final three choices, but he knew all along he would become a Cane, just like his cousin Donald "Duck" Ellis.

"Miami was a bigger learning curve," German said. "Miami was overwhelming to me. I didn't have Coach Sam anymore. I was really letting loose. The spotlight, the stadium. I'm walking through Publix one day. In Miami. I'm at the magazine rack, looking at hip-hop magazines. I look to the left, and I see myself on the front of the college sports magazine. My picture was huge. I'm on the cover. And I look at the other one. I'm on the cover of that one, too!

"That's a lot to handle for a young man. My head got a little too big. I didn't take all that too well."

As a sophomore at Miami, German had 159 receiving yards and 2 touchdowns against Arizona State. Things were looking good on the field, and sometimes they seemed even better off it.

"It wasn't a college town," German said of Miami. "It's an NFL town. When we come out of the game, we're going to South Beach, partying, and the big boys took care of you. It was too much for me to handle."

German caught a combined 49 passes for 604 yards and 3 touchdowns as a freshman and sophomore. He led the Hurricanes with 41 catches for 730 yards, finishing with 3 touchdowns as a junior in 1995.

Ready to break out as a senior, German tore the two major ligaments in his left knee in the spring of 1996. He received a medical redshirt, allowing him to sit out the season without losing a year of eligibility. But he also received scrutiny from the NCAA for violating rules. German had taken a free limousine ride and eaten a dinner paid for by an agent. By doing so, he lost that final year of eligibility in 1997.

German said he took the limo ride because at the time, he had planned on turning pro anyway. After Ohio State's Terry Glenn, USC's Keyshawn Johnson, and Syracuse's Marvin Harrison all declared themselves eligible for the NFL Draft following their junior seasons, German realized his error too late.

"I decided to stay in school and try to go top five the next year," German said. "It backfired, because I did take extra benefits."

German then dug his hole even deeper. He lied to the NCAA during the investigation. "I lied because I was scared," German said. "I was scared I was going to lose my eligibility."

The Atlanta Falcons, which had drafted Sanders and Walter Sutton in years past, selected German in the third round as the seventy-fourth overall pick in the 1998 NFL Draft. That third-round selection caught even German off-guard.

"Street sense, book sense, and common sense," said German, who believed he aced his performances at the NFL Scouting Combine, the annual showcase for professional football prospects. "You've got to have all three. If you got all three, you're good."

German finished three of his four NFL seasons on the injured reserve list. He finished his NFL career with 20 catches for 294 yards and 3 touchdowns.

Two of those touchdowns German scored on December 19, 1999. German caught 3 passes for 35 yards and the 2 scores for the Falcons on the road against the Tennessee Titans. The Titans had a six-foot, 4-inch, 265-pound, freakish defensive end, also from Fort Myers, in the starting lineup that day. This player never enjoyed the two-parent household that German did. Jevon Kearse never even knew his father.

Robert "Pompey" Green, the first African-American athlete from Fort Myers to try out for an NFL team, had his number retired in 2008 at Dunbar
High School. Photo courtesy of the *News-Press*.

Robert "Pompey" Green, shown here circa 1949 in uniform for the Dunbar Tigers, went on to play on scholarship at Allen University in South Carolina. Photo courtesy of the *News-Press*.

Mario Henderson, who started at offensive tackle in twenty-eight games over four seasons with the Oakland Raiders, only played one season of varsity football at Lehigh Senior High School. Photo by Marc Beaudin.

Noel Devine, who went on to play at West Virginia University after setting the Lee County record for rushing yardage, makes a move on a defender. Photo by John David Emmett.

Terrence Cody signed with Mississippi Gulf Coast Community College out of Riverdale High School before playing for Alabama and then in the NFL with the Baltimore Ravens. Photo by Kim Hart.

Terrence Cody goes up against the Lely High School defense when he appeared as a running back at Riverdale High School. Photo by Amanda Inscore.

Jevon Kearse hugs his mother, Lessie Green, upon being drafted as a defensive end by the Tennessee Titans in the 1999 NFL Draft. Kearse played at the University of Florida and North Fort Myers High School. Photo by K. T. Warnke.

Earnest Graham (*right*) and Brandon Graham pose for a portrait during their days as teammates and fellow running backs at Mariner High School. Earnest Graham went on to play eight seasons for the Tampa Bay Buccaneers; Brandon Graham went on to receive a five-year prison sentence for selling drugs. Photo by K. T. Warnke.

Earnest Graham (*left*) and Anthony Henry, who each went on to play in the NFL, hug one another upon being inducted into the Lee County High School Sports Hall of Fame. The two shared an apartment in Dunbar for a time as children. Photo by Todd Stubing.

Deion Sanders poses at his 2011 Pro Football Hall of Fame induction with his bronze bust after placing a blue do-rag on it. Sanders, a North Fort Myers High School graduate, played for fourteen seasons in the NFL with five teams. Photo by John David Emmett.

Deion Sanders (number 29) runs for yardage in his days as a Pop Warner football player for the Fort Myers Rebels, circa 1978. Sanders autographed this photo and gave it to his coach, Dave Capel. Photo courtesy of Helen Capel.

Sammy Watkins, who grew up not far from where his great-grandfather was murdered, ended up being Lee County's all-time leading receiver at South Fort Myers High before playing at Clemson University and becoming an NFL Draft pick. At age seventeen, he poses holding a football with his family: mother Nicole McMiller, father James McMiller, brother Jari McMiller and, in the front, sisters Markeisha (*left*) and Mykelah McMiller. Photo by Lindsay Terry.

Sammy Watkins celebrates the signing of his letter of intent with Clemson University, three years before preparing for the NFL Draft. Photo by Lindsay Terry.

Sammy Watkins races away from defenders in the John Carrigan Rotary South All-Star Classic following his senior season at South Fort Myers, three years before declaring for the NFL Draft out of Clemson University. Photo by Kinfay Moroti.

Tampa Bay Buccaneers running back Earnest Graham with his fifteen-month-old son Earnest Myles, four-year-old daughter Aiyana, and wife, Alicia, on June 8, 2007, in Tampa, Florida. Photo by John David Emmett.

Earnest Graham leaves the St. Louis Rams defense behind him on his way to the end zone for the Tampa Bay Buccaneers on September 23, 2007, at Raymond James Stadium in Tampa. Photo by John David Emmett.

Kearse  10

Jevon Kearse could not find his chocolate milk. For an eighth-grader, this could be considered a crisis. Kearse, tall for his age and skinny, had gotten up from the table and grabbed something else to eat in the Lee Middle School cafeteria.

"I came back," Kearse said, "and the chocolate milk was missing. I'm like, 'Where's my chocolate milk?'"

The tone within Kearse's teenaged mind transformed from curiosity to anger. He saw fellow eighth-grader Cisco Navas sitting nearby, holding a carton of chocolate milk. Kearse believed it to be his. Navas and Kearse vaguely knew one another from playing Pop Warner football.

"He said that I took his chocolate milk," said Navas, who ended up being a teammate of Kearse and a bulldog of a fullback at North Fort Myers High School. "But it was my chocolate milk."

"I went after Cisco and grabbed him," Kearse said. "He fell into his chair."

"I think I beat him up," Navas said. "That's my claim to fame. I slammed him, and he slammed me back. I don't know if he was just making that up to get my milk or what."

The lunch-duty teachers broke up the fight. The principal brought Navas and Kearse with him to his office.

"We concocted a story that we were just playing," Kearse said. "We said we were just wrestling. We knew each other from Pop Warner, and we were just joking around. The principal was like, 'Are you sure?'"

The incident united Kearse and Navas, who became fast friends. Their friendship might have saved Kearse's life.

The odds for Jevon Kearse to succeed were not good, not if you knew the fates of his father and grandfather. Jevon Kearse lived on Dora Street in the housing project east of the railroad tracks in Fort Myers, west of Ford Street and just south of Edison Avenue. He grew up in the heart of Dunbar in the Old Projects, officially named Southward Village.

Born on September 3, 1976, Jevon Kearse entered the world seven years after Lee County public schools were desegregated. In the mid-1970s, most of Lee County's African Americans still lived in Dunbar. There were about thirty thousand Fort Myers residents in 1976. Of that number, about three thousand were African Americans. Most of them were Christian, but they worshipped at different churches from their white counterparts. They shopped at different grocery stores, ate at different restaurants, uniting one day a week. They gathered to watch high school football games at Cape Coral, Cypress Lake, Fort Myers, North Fort Myers, and Riverdale High Schools.

The mid- to late 1970s were tumultuous times for anyone in Fort Myers named Kearse. The family stood tall in stature and large in number. Jevon Kearse had four aunts and eight uncles. The shortest of the boys were five foot eleven, but three of them grew to six foot three, six foot four, and six foot five.

"There's something in their blood," said Brenda Kearse, who married Jevon's uncle Paul. "If they ever got cut, it would heal in just a few days. None of my kids ever needed any medical treatment. There's just something in that bloodline. If the family members just took care of themselves? They could live long and healthy and happy lives."

Not enough of the Kearses did that.

Joseph Kearse Sr., the seventh-youngest child of George Kearse, lived on Dora Street in Southward Village on the same block on which his sons Joseph Jr. and Jevon would be raised. Joseph Kearse Sr. had a two-page arrest record that began in 1964, when he was twelve years old. He once received immunity in a murder case from State Attorney Joseph D'Alessandro in exchange for testimony against others.

Heroin already had hit Dunbar during that time, and the "reefer," or marijuana, had just begun to infiltrate the streets.

Years before Jevon Kearse fought Cisco Navas over chocolate milk and before Jevon Kearse attained his nickname "The Freak," Joseph Kearse Sr. had fought for his life and dealt with the offensive nickname "Gorilla." In 1976, Lee County sheriff's deputies called Joseph Kearse Sr. that name. Built like his then-unborn son Jevon would be at six foot four, Joseph Kearse Sr. had a reputation as a "shakedown artist," a man who took money from dope peddlers, gamblers, and drunks, wrote reporter Lee Melsek in the *News-Press*.

"If Kearse had two friends, he had two thousand enemies," one unnamed lawman told Melsek.

Navas and another one of Jevon's childhood friends, Joe Lewis, had heard of Joseph Kearse Sr.'s reputation, some of which had become distorted over time. They shared their impressions in a *Sports Illustrated* profile of Jevon Kearse, written by Michael Silver and published April 28, 2000, at the beginning of Kearse's NFL dominance with the Tennessee Titans.

"People say Jevon's dad was a bad, bad man," Navas said. "Word was, he used to rob people with his bare hands."

Said Lewis: "Yeah, he'd just turn 'em upside down and take their change if he had to."

A masked gunman ended all of that. He shot Joseph Kearse Sr. in the throat on February 1, 1976, at Brown's Pool Hall in Fort Myers. A few days prior, Kearse Sr. had knocked out a migrant farmworker in a dispute over a dice game. They were gambling, and Kearse Sr. just may have gambled away his life by knocking the man unconscious, for that man was believed to be the murderer.

"Joe Kearse took a lot of money from a lot of people, and maybe one of them just got fed up with it," a police officer told Melsek in the 1976 *News-Press*. "Whoever did it got awful brave."

Joseph Kearse Sr. died the next day at Lee Memorial Hospital. He was twenty-four.

"The people in Dunbar are funny about things like this," State Attorney D'Alessandro told Melsek following the murder. Years later, Jevon Kearse would work for D'Alessandro as an office assistant when spending his summers in Fort Myers between school years as a football player at the University of Florida.

"If they think a wrong has been done, they will cooperate with us and help us find the guilty party," D'Alessandro told Melsek. "But if they think justice has been served by something like this, they'll just clam up and refuse to talk to us."

The cops never brought Joseph Kearse's killer to justice.

Eight months and two days after his father's murder, Jevon Kearse entered the world as the second-born son of Joseph Kearse Sr. His firstborn son, Joseph Kearse Jr., then two, would grow up having only the vaguest of memory of his father.

"I can remember him walking me across the street and pointing the way for me to walk to Grandma's house," said Joseph Kearse Jr., whose son Jayron Kearse would grow up to become a Clemson University safety after graduating from South Fort Myers High School in 2013. "I can remember that. But every time I try to turn around and look at my father, I can't see him. I can never see his face."

The murder began shaping the Kearse family's reputation for the worse. The family name rhymed with "fierce" in parts of South Carolina. In Fort Myers, the name always sounded like "curse."

Joseph Kearse Sr.'s life never should have ended that way, his brother Paul Kearse said. If it hadn't, the "shakedown artist" label never would have stuck. The urban legend of Joseph Kearse Sr. living like a 1970s Robin Hood, stealing from drug dealers in order to provide for his family, never would have happened, either.

"He was no angel," Paul Kearse said. "But he was a dedicated family man. Joe was a man who had the athletic ability. But during that time, schools were still desegregating. When they did integrate the schools, he went out for football."

Upon trying out for the Fort Myers High School football team, Joseph Kearse Sr. did not have the right kind of socks. An assistant coach chewed him out, telling him not to bring with him a negative attitude.

"My brother felt like he wasn't going to get a fair shake," Paul Kearse said. "He quit the team. Eventually, he quit school. My other older brother James, he quit school, too. At that time, education wasn't a priority in my family. I looked around, and I saw how everything was. I knew there had to be something better than what I was seeing. I knew if I had an education, that doors would open."

While Paul Kearse settled in Tampa, things deteriorated in Dunbar, especially for the Kearse family. According to stories published in the *News-Press*:

On February 5, 1978, George Kearse, fifty-seven years old and Jevon Kearse's paternal grandfather, was murdered outside his home on Ben Street, shot with a .22 caliber, nickel-plated handgun. Police found him lying on his back and cradling a shotgun in his right arm. Someone had shot him in the chest.

On July 23, 1978, Danny Kearse, nineteen years old and one of Jevon's cousins, was shot in the right temple and killed on Franklin Street by a snow-cone vendor named Ronald Blum, who wielded a .357 Magnum. A grand jury ruled the shooting self-defense.

On January 26, 1980, James Kearse, thirty years old and one of Jevon's uncles, was shot through the heart and killed. He was the fourth member of the family to die from a gunshot in four years.

Paul Kearse came close to witnessing that murder, having driven back to his hometown that day.

"I saw a crowd gathering," Paul Kearse said. "I said to my wife, we were in the car, 'Somebody has probably done something stupid.' By the time I got to my mother's house, they told me that James had gotten shot."

Emotions ran high when Paul Kearse arrived at the site of his brother's body.

"There was no need to let him lay out there like that," Paul Kearse said. "I started fussing. They told me that if I don't close my mouth, they would take me to jail for disorderly conduct. One of the police got me off to the side and was talking to me while this was going on. The coroner finally came, and they pronounced him dead.

"I expected James to die. James, he was a *Jesse* James. One time my mother told me that somebody had told her he had gotten into a gun battle. They were shooting at each other like cowboys in a western."

Not just the shootings, but the boorish behavior by many of his friends in Dunbar motivated Paul Kearse to leave Fort Myers for Tampa, where he loaded and drove trucks for a living, later finding a job as an insurance inspector. In the 1970s, Paul Kearse saw his friends spending weeknights, in addition to Fridays and Saturdays, barhopping between the Hi Tech, Club 82, and L.M. nightclubs. If his friends were not drunk or high, they were living aimlessly. The barhopping scene ended Paul Kearse's thoughts of returning home other than to visit.

"I started to hear about classmates getting shot because of the drugs," Paul Kearse said. "Then they were robbing the drug lords. Then the drug lords would put a hit on the robbers. Ricky Hixon was one of my classmates. He was the first one of my classmates to die. He must have died in late '73 or early '74. They told me he took somebody's drugs, and I don't know what it was that he took, and he ran. He was jumping a ditch, and they shot him in the back. From my understanding, the guy who shot him didn't get any time for shooting him, because he was an informant for the police."

In January 1981, Marcell Kearse of Dora Street, one of Jevon's cousins, was charged with attempted murder and later sentenced to twelve years in prison. He was nineteen. He had drug, battery, armed robbery, and grand theft auto charges on his record and died in 1997 in a prison hospital.

"I've had my heart full," Pauline Kearse, the wife of James and an aunt of Jevon, told the *News-Press*. She had lost a husband, two sons, a daughter, and a nephew to gunshots.

"The Kearse family is tired of being shot down in Fort Myers," Georgia Kearse, one of Jevon's aunts, said to the *News-Press*. "That's five already. We can't go for six. The buck has got to stop somewhere. I just do not want this to go down like it did with my other brother. He was no gorilla."

On March 19, 1991, Robert Kearse Jr., sixteen years old and one of Jevon's cousins, received a sentence of life in prison, with no possibility of parole for twenty-five years. Court records showed him guilty of a May 16, 1990, shooting and robbery in which he killed twenty-year-old

Christopher Jennings on Economy Street. Before that, Robert Kearse Jr. had been arrested on seven felony charges.

"I would say to you that sending you to prison for a long time might save your life," Lee Circuit Judge William Nelson said in the courtroom. "It's a vicious cycle I don't know how to stop. It's a useless thing."

In the fall of 1995, Jevon Kearse's first year at the University of Florida, the freshman ended up spending a night in jail. Kearse was accused of stealing a car in Sarasota County several months earlier. The police in Gainesville ran a background check on Kearse after coming to his apartment for a noise complaint. Kearse had been playing his radio too loud. During his night in jail, Kearse realized what had happened, that his older brother and father's namesake, Joseph Kearse Jr., had stolen the car and given police Jevon's name upon being arrested. Joseph Kearse Jr. later received a seven-year sentence for armed robbery. By 2013, he had left crime behind, and he attended many of his son Jayron's high school games.

In October 1996, another Kearse was murdered. Jermaine Kearse, one of Jevon's younger brothers and better known as "Rocky," was shot and killed during Jevon's sophomore year at the University of Florida. Two cars pulled into the Sabal Palms apartment complex in Dunbar. Men jumped out and shot Rocky to death. Jevon Kearse has a tattoo of him on his shoulder that shows a cross with rose vines on it and his brother's initials. "FATHER FORGIVE ME FOR I HAVE SINNED," is written on it. Jevon Kearse later named his dog after Rocky.

Not even after moving to Tampa could Paul Kearse and his family escape the violence.

On January 7, 2010, George Kearse, the son of Paul and Brenda Kearse and a first cousin to Jevon, was shot and killed near his Tampa home. Home for winter break after finishing a football season for Benedict College in South Carolina, George Kearse ended up in the wrong place at the wrong time. Like the murdered grandfather he never knew, George Kearse died at age twenty-four.

The murder of their son prompted Brenda Kearse to start writing a book, tentatively titled *Consequences of Crime: It's Your Move.*

"I was a center," Brenda Kearse said of her basketball-playing days. "Which means you get challenged all the time. The center controls the basket. One thing I learned: You come into my territory, I'm going to wait on you. You might get me the first time. You might knock me down. That window of opportunity, I'm going to get my lick in."

Brenda Kearse intended to get her book into the hands of at-risk juveniles.

"This generation of children, they're video-game kids," Brenda Kearse said. "Checkers and chess, they're really a thinking man's games. You have to think of the consequences before you act on them. If you take this move, then this will happen. Teenagers now are not thinking about consequences.

"I've lost one. I'm hoping I can save at least one."

The positive influences of Jevon Kearse's friends and aunts and uncles saved Jevon from so many of his other family members' fates. Jevon Kearse rewarded them by transforming the family name from one feared and shunned into one respected and celebrated. Jevon Kearse began that transformation by studying hard, working hard, and becoming one of the NFL's most feared pass rushers. The Tennessee Titans selected Kearse in the first round of the NFL Draft in 1999 with the sixteenth overall pick following his junior season at Florida.

Possessing a pair of the most massive hands anyone ever would see, Jevon Kearse earned his nickname, the "Freak," also because of his six-foot, four-inch, 265-pound frame, his 4.43-second 40-yard dash time, and his incredible wingspan. His arms, spread wide, measured a little more than seven feet across from fingertip to fingertip. A foot-long ruler would just about fit between his outstretched pinky and thumb.

Jevon Kearse did his best to put an end to the cycle of violence. By 1991, thirteen-year-old Jevon Kearse had survived the chaos around him and his family. At that age, he already considered himself the man of the house. He had one older brother, four younger brothers, and a sister.

Jevon Kearse took care of his younger siblings most days, getting them ready for school and helping them after school while their mother, Lessie Green, worked.

"I did a lot of growing up for myself," Jevon Kearse said. "There were a lot of influences around me. It taught me responsibility early. From elementary school on, I was babysitting my younger siblings and getting their food ready to eat."

Following Lee Middle School, Jevon Kearse enrolled at Fort Myers High School, where he played freshman football. Kearse had followed the Fort Myers Green Wave teams of the early 1990s, including one of the best teams—if not the best—in Lee County history. Coached by Sam Sirianni Sr., the 1991–92 Green Wave had Jammi German, plus loads of other Division I college talent, including defensive back/wide receiver Nod Washington, who later would see fame as a rapper known as Plies.

"I was using my mom's boyfriend's address," Jevon Kearse said of how he ended up at Fort Myers as a freshman. "Fort Myers was really good, but I got tired of wearing jeans at school. At North, you could wear shorts. I didn't really care about the football team then."

Fort Myers coach Sam Sirianni Jr. recalled a different scene. According to Sirianni, his father saw Kearse crying in one of the school's hallways upon learning he would have to transfer to North Fort Myers following his freshman year.

"Let me tell you something, Jevon," Sam Sirianni Sr. said, according to his son. "You're going to do just fine. No matter where you end up, you're going to be successful."

As a sophomore at North Fort Myers, Kearse reunited with Navas, who was becoming a good football player in his own right as a linebacker and fullback. They hit it off as friends, having put the chocolate milk incident behind them.

Jevon began spending more and more time with Cisco, at his rural home near the interstate. Navas's family owned several acres of land, and Cisco Navas did not live in a neighborhood full of gunfire, stabbings, and drug deals. Kearse eventually moved in with Navas.

"He would sit in the living room and do his homework," Navas said. "No one ever told him to do his homework. You know what? To this day, I always tell my kids about Jevon doing his homework. I say, 'Uncle Von always did it. Nobody ever told him to.'"

Navas does not believe he saved Kearse from getting into trouble and straying from the right path. Kearse saved himself, Navas said.

"By meeting him and him moving into my house, it definitely helped," Navas said. "But at the same time, Jevon's not a follower. He has always been a leader, no matter what he does. If he wants to do something, he'll do it. If he doesn't, he'll let you know."

At North Fort Myers High, that type of attitude sometimes got Kearse into then-coach Wade Hummel's doghouse. Navas and Kearse had car problems throughout their sophomore season. Hummel grew tired of them using the car as an excuse, telling Kearse not to even bother coming back for the final game of his sophomore season.

"The end of my sophomore year really motivated me," Kearse said. "Me and Cisco got only one letter from college. We each got a letter from Florida State. That was big. That was big-time right there. It really motivated me. I showed everybody. I wish I still had it. But it got lost."

Hummel and Kearse worked out their differences.

"That same summer, Coach Hummel ended up getting us jobs at New Life Fitness Center," Kearse said. "We'd have to clean up a little bit, but then we would work out, play basketball, go swimming or whatever."

Ron Hoover, who coached Deion Sanders at North Fort Myers before moving back to his native Missouri for several years, had heard of Kearse from afar. Hoover eventually returned to North Fort Myers High and became an assistant to Hummel before retiring to his home on Pine Island, a fishing paradise about a forty-minute drive west of the high school. Hummel suffered a stroke in 2008 and died in March 2012.

"I told Wade I was coming back from Missouri," said Hoover, who was an assistant coach for five seasons in Warsaw, Missouri. "We won the state championship up there. When I told him I was coming back, he asked me if I'd do the offense. He said, 'Wait until you see Jevon and what an athlete he is.' I always compared him to a big Deion Sanders. When we had our seven-on-seven games, and he was playing safety— the way he could get up in the air? God Almighty, he could jump. He could cover ground like no one else, the way he could get up in the air."

Kearse played safety on defense and tight end on offense. Kearse did not play enough offense, to either his liking or to Hoover's.

"I'll tell you what," Hoover said of a North Fort Myers playoff run that ended in Fort Lauderdale. "We played St. Thomas Aquinas his senior year. They had a little cornerback who was covering him. He was like five foot ten, and Jevon was like six foot four. When I look back on it, we could have thrown it to Jevon on a quick hitch and let him go one-on-one with the little cornerback. We could have just watched him go."

"We were down on the goal line, first and goal," Kearse recalled of his last high school game. "I'm at wide receiver, and we didn't score. The guy covering me was like this tall," he said, spreading his index finger and thumb apart.

"I did great at safety," Kearse said. "One of the biggest plays I made was against Fort Myers. Fort Myers was talking smack. They had a quarterback, David Travis. I had, like, three or four backpedals, and the ball was coming toward me, but high, over my head. I jumped up and grabbed it, one-handed, fully extended. I landed on my back, like a back flop. I got up, like, 'Hell yeah!' That's when I realized I was start- ing to be pretty good. We won almost all of our games by a bunch of touchdowns."

The Red Knights finished with a 12–1 record that year, best in school history. By then, that one recruiting letter after his sophomore season had blossomed into shoeboxes full of mail.

Kearse, listed then at six foot, four inches and 220 pounds, carried a 3.6 grade-point average. He was named first-team All-State and won the Lee County Sportsmen Club's Most Valuable Player Award and the Rotary South Club's Scholar Athlete Award.

The time had arrived for Kearse to choose a college. He became the first male figure in his immediate family to make such a choice.

Kearse visited Florida State unofficially, traveling there with Navas. Kearse then took official visits to Miami, Ohio State, Notre Dame, and Florida.

Miami, Kearse said, seemed too good to be true.

"I went to my first strip club down there," Kearse said. "Every place you would go, there was love. I knew I couldn't go there."

Kearse admitted to not being very interested in Ohio State, but he wanted to take advantage of the free trip. So he took it.

"I took the Ohio State visit just to see snow for the first time," he said. "I could have gone up there and fallen in love with it."

Instead?

"I went up there and made my first snowball."

Kearse canceled an official visit to Florida State, instead going to Notre Dame.

"I was blown away by their tradition," he said. "I committed when I was up there. I was fully committed to going there."

Kearse almost canceled his scheduled official visit to the University of Florida. Having enjoyed all of his other visits, he decided to follow through and visit the Gainesville campus.

"As soon as I got to Florida, that was it," Kearse said. "It wasn't too far from home—or far enough."

On a Wednesday morning in February 1995, Kearse made official his decision to play for the Gators, furthering his path to the NFL. At about the same time, another high-powered player from Dunbar ascended to the throne of high school football in Lee County.

Anthony Ascends

Anthony Henry had to get rich in order to understand what it meant to be poor.

Unlike many of the children who grew up in his Dunbar neighborhood, Henry never idolized money or had a *Scarface* movie poster on his wall. He never wore T-shirts with dollar-bill signs or got gold caps on his teeth. He did not at first even aspire to play in the NFL.

"Anthony was one of my kids that they called a mama's boy," said his mother, Essie Mae Robinson, who answers to Mae. "He never went anywhere. He never spent the night at anybody's house when he was a kid. He always made sure I was around.

"I used to always say, 'Anthony, you're going to be a real wimp.' He would cry about everything. He would get a cut on his fingers or an ant bite, and he would cry. I used to think there was no way he could play football, because he was a little wimp.

"We were surprised that he even went to college. He always told me that when he got older, he was going to take care of me. And I always said, 'Yeah, right.' I told him, 'You've got to work hard in school.' And he really, really did. He really came through for me."

Born on November 3, 1976, the son of Alto Henry Sr. and Robinson, the future cornerback for the Cleveland Browns, Dallas Cowboys, and Detroit Lions grew up in Michigan Court, one of the roughest and toughest of the Fort Myers housing projects. In the 1980s, Dunbar residents referred to Michigan Court by a simple nickname, "The Hood." Drug deals were rampant, and police could do little to stop them. There was only one way in and one way out of "The Hood." News of approaching police spread Paul Revere–style, as fast as the legs and bicycles of teenagers could carry them. The city demolished Michigan Court in 2001.

Henry's mother, a graduate of segregated Dunbar High, often worked two jobs as she raised her two sons and daughter. Anthony Henry later moved his mother into a three-bedroom home in Lehigh Acres, a comfortable but not extravagant house he bought for $250,000. At Christmastime each year, Mae filled the house from one end to the other with stuffed Santas, nativity scenes, and other decorations, turning her house into a winter wonderland.

Anthony Henry's father, Alto Henry Sr., was born in 1943 in Eufaula, a seaport town in southeast Alabama, near the Georgia border. He moved to Fort Myers at age fifteen in 1958, attending Dunbar High and working as a roofer and farmer.

"It was pretty rough back then, yes it was," Mae Robinson said of living conditions in the late 1950s and 1960s. She walked three miles to school every day, living off Anderson Avenue.

"In the day, I'd worked on the farms, picking tomatoes and collard greens and all sorts of stuff," she said. "At night, I worked at the Lee County Justice Center, cleaning. I sacrificed in any way in order to feed my kids."

Robinson taught her children to know right from wrong, to praise the Lord, and to stay out of trouble. She succeeded on all three counts with two of her three children, but not with her oldest son. Alto Henry Jr. never played high school football, and he ended up getting into trouble numerous times. He had been in and out of jails and prisons since 1991. His downward spiral began with an accident. At age nine, Alto suffered severe burns when he nearly electrocuted himself. Playing outside, Alto sat on top of a transformer box that the power company had been working on that day. An exposed live wire burned him.

The near-electrocution did more than scar Alto. "He was never quite right after that," Robinson said of the power line accident. Alto Henry Jr. had his nickname, Kilo Watt Lightning Bolt, tattooed across his stomach. His rap sheet included arson, burglary, robbery, grand theft, and cocaine possession and dealing.

Anthony Henry, who declined to talk about his brother, stayed clear of those pitfalls and stayed close to his mother. Alto Henry Sr. remained involved in his life but from out of the house.

"Me and my dad have a great relationship," Anthony Henry said. "We didn't grow up in the same household. But I would see my dad. He's one of my best friends. I can talk to him about anything. My mom never talked down on him. She always said she loved him, no matter what the situation."

Not having his father at home meant Henry had to grow up fast. He lived around crime and had to avoid becoming prey to it.

"I've seen people get shot," Anthony Henry said of living in Michigan Court. "I've seen people get stabbed. I've seen all the drugs. I've seen all that stuff. It wasn't even my mom saying don't do this or don't do that. Of course she said that. But I didn't want to be in those situations. I want to say it had to be God. I got offered to sell drugs, a number of times. But I didn't. I made a lot of simple mistakes. But at that point in my life growing up, that wasn't one of them. Once you go down that road, it's hard to come back from that."

In 1996, Henry made his first step toward becoming a University of South Florida Hall of Famer by becoming one of the first recruits in that football program's history. Until that time, Henry worked multiple jobs, not because he wanted the money, but because his family needed it. As a child, Anthony often walked with his mother from Michigan Court three miles to downtown Fort Myers, where he helped her clean law offices on the weekends. As a teenager, Anthony worked as a busboy at the Farmer's Market restaurant in Fort Myers and at the Fort Myers Kmart, squeezing the hours around his football, basketball, and track and field practices.

"Until I started going to Bonita Middle and Cypress Middle School, when I started having friends who were white, I didn't understand how little money we had," Henry said. "One of my friends, I would go to his house, and he even had a pool. The funny thing is I didn't even know the difference. Now looking back, I realize how bad it was. But when you're in the situation, you don't realize what it is. Everyone out there was in the same situation."

Mae Robinson struggled when asked of Anthony's biggest instance of violating her rules. One time, she brought home a brand-new bottle of her favorite perfume. Anthony, then eight years old, sprayed the entire bottle all over the house while his mother was working.

"I can't think of anything else," Mae Robinson said. "That's the worst thing he's ever done."

Anthony Henry, however, confessed to one other crime.

As a freshman at Estero High School, he quit going to Sunday school. After throwing four interceptions against Lehigh in the season opener of his senior season, Henry decided to attend church again.

"I didn't think things could get worse than that," Henry told the *News-Press* as a nineteen-year-old in 1996. From then on, including throughout his lucrative NFL career, Henry said he tithed 10 percent of his income to various churches. "I knew there was something I needed to do if I wanted to improve my life."

The rest of Henry's senior season at Estero, he threw just two more interceptions. He completed 49 of 108 passes for 821 yards and 7 touchdowns. He rushed 84 times for 534 yards and 7 touchdowns. He even led Lee County in punting with a 40.6-yard average. In Lee County's All-Star high school football game for seniors, later known as the John Carrigan Rotary South All-Star Classic, Henry scored on a 62-yard run in the first quarter and had a 17-yard interception return in the third quarter, leading his South team to a 19–9 victory. Henry earned his team's most valuable player award.

In basketball, Henry averaged 12.3 points and 8.3 rebounds per game.

"He just had the ability to disrupt people," Estero basketball coach Lee Peters said of Henry, particularly on the defensive side of the game. "That was a major part of his success. And there were some individual dunks that were pretty impressive. One time, he came out of nowhere.

It looked like he took off from ten feet away from the basket and just went over everybody."

Henry also used that athleticism in track and field. As a six-foot, one-inch, 175-pound senior, Henry qualified for the Class 5A state meet, placing fifth in the triple jump and seventh in the long jump.

"I feel like he has achieved so many things concerning sports," Mae Robinson said. "But the most important thing he has done is reach all of the goals he's wanted to reach. He never wanted to miss not one day of school."

Henry also had a male figure mentoring him in Estero football coach Joe Hampton. Hampton became the first Lee County public school coach to lead a team to a state championship game in 1998, when Estero fell to Kissimmee Osceola High 28–14 two years after Henry graduated. Before that, Hampton and then assistant coach Anthony Dixon, another black athlete born and raised in Michigan Court, helped transform Henry into a young man with the potential for greatness.

Making It in Michigan Court

When the Lee County School District sliced Dunbar like a pie, dividing its student-athletes among the integrated schools, Michigan Court eventually served as a feeder for Estero High.

Dixon, Sammy Brown, and Mike Sturgis, all longtime residents of Michigan Court and neighbors of Anthony Henry, were zoned for Estero as products of "The Hood." Dixon, Brown, and Sturgis reflected upon their upbringing and how it shaped them for the better.

Drug pushers who saw athletic potential in Michigan Court teenagers would steer them away from "the life."

"If I showed up on the corner and tried to hang out, they wouldn't let me," Dixon said. "A lot of times, they wouldn't be very friendly to me, and a lot of times, my family would hear about it the next day. So I could only assume what they were doing out there. If they felt like you had a future, then they would go above and beyond to protect you."

The code of the streets since has changed for the worse.

"Nowadays, they're more like putting it in their hands," Dixon said of the drugs. "But back then, we were pretty much representing our neighborhood. We were making a good statement. We showed that we had guys who were going to school every day and doing the right thing. The younger generation, they got away from that. Now you have people growing up in so many different places. But back at Michigan Court, that was the only type of lifestyle that the people knew. A lot of people would never even leave Michigan Court unless it was to go to work or go to school."

Dixon, destined to play wide receiver at Marshall University and in the Arena Football League after graduating from Estero in 1994, grew up in the single-parent home of his aunt. His father lived in Fort Pierce, Florida, and his mother moved from Michigan Court to the Sabal Palms housing projects, prompting Dixon to move in with his aunt and two cousins so that he would not have to switch elementary schools.

Curtis Hood Sr., the older brother of future Tampa Bay Buccaneers practice squad member and Cape Coral High School graduate Ed Gant, took dozens of children under his wing during Dixon's formative years. Hood would drive them from Michigan Court to Pop Warner football practice with the Riverdale Wildcats until he was murdered, stabbed to death in 1988 in Dunbar.

Frankie Raybon, an uncle to future NFL cornerback Phillip Buchanon and brother to Gant, said if his oldest brother had not died, even more Fort Myers–raised athletes probably would have reached the NFL.

"It was a tragic death," Raybon said. "That's what really hurt. He wasn't that kind of a guy to get in trouble. He was in the wrong place at the wrong time. That's what I would say. He's a guy who would have fifteen, sixteen kids in his car taking kids to Pop Warner football practice. This was back in 1982."

Sammy Brown, Estero High class of 1993 and the defensive coordinator at integrated Dunbar High in 2014, focused on the positives while growing up in Michigan Court.

"Michigan, it was home, you know what I'm saying?" Brown said. "When I came to Michigan, a lot of people from the outside thought it was a horrific place. For me, I knew it as a place where all of my buddies were at. For me, it was home.

"It had some crime in it. When you're on the outside, that's all you read about. You don't know the final result and how it happened. In the end, I'm telling you, we saw a light at the end of the tunnel. We just made it work. You've got to punch the code to go into the gate. My mom and dad, they did everything they could do for me. My dad was a block mason. My mom worked in a retirement home. There were constant reminders in my household of what to do, what's right, what's wrong. The kids who make it out, all of their moms would say the same things. Educate yourself. You heard it religiously. Everywhere you went. And Coach Hampton, he'd always lead us the right way."

Mike Sturgis, Estero High class of 2002 and a first cousin of Anthony Henry, was younger than Henry, Dixon, and Brown. The Michigan Court housing projects spanned all of Sturgis's childhood.

"They tore it down when I went off to college," said Sturgis, who went to Hutchinson Community College in Kansas, Georgia Military College, and Murray State from 2005 to 2007. The second-oldest of four children, Sturgis did not have a father in the home. His mother worked three jobs, including one at a nursing home. With his parents either absent or busy, Sturgis fended for himself.

"I saw everything, man," Sturgis said of his upbringing. "I saw drugs. I saw people getting shot. I saw the whole nine, bro. I had to grow up quick and fast because of the environment I was in. People knew I didn't want to go down that road. Some of my best friends sold drugs. I never wanted to do that. I saw the good from the bad. I saw what happened to them."

Sturgis also saw the value in sports.

"You always had something to look forward to as far as playing basketball, racing somebody, playing football," he said. "Even though it was a bad neighborhood, you always had a lot of good competition out there. It taught me not to be afraid of nothing."

Sturgis played football against older children. They knocked the wind out of him on a regular basis. They toughened him.

"I wasn't afraid as a young kid," said Sturgis, who was described by former Estero teammate Matt Prater as the hardest-hitting safety he had ever seen. That included Prater's time spent at the University of Central Florida and in the NFL, mostly with the Denver Broncos as the team's placekicker.

"It taught me a lot," Sturgis said of playing football in "The Hood." "It taught me to be brave. You're going through so much. You see so much. You can't be afraid."

Sturgis learned to channel any fears into aggression on the football field. "I had a lot of anger in me, to protect myself and my teammates. They were like family to me."

Sturgis endured an injury-plagued junior season at Murray State, combined with a falling-out with his coach as a senior. That limited his professional football opportunities. With the impending birth of his daughter, Sturgis returned to Fort Myers seeking employment. He found it as a security guard, first at Estero High and then at Island Coast High School in Cape Coral. When he moved back home, the reality of Michigan Court being demolished hit him.

"I was devastated," Sturgis said. "That's where all my friends grew up. That's where I had a lot of memories, living in my apartment. You can't just take something away like that. I was really disappointed it got knocked down. Then again, I was happy it got knocked down, because of all the violence there. Something was happening every day. The police were out there every day. People needed a change."

Henry Helped by Hampton

When Anthony Henry needed to change from an unknown freshman high school player to a future NFL prospect, he sought Coach Hampton's guidance. Henry found a father figure in Hampton, who used to give Henry rides home from practice, a thirty-minute drive from Estero.

Many of the young black athletes from Dunbar who did not fall into the street life had older white male role models who looked out for them. Deion Sanders had two in Dave Capel and Ron Hoover. Eric Riley had two in Sam Sirianni Sr. and Hampton. Jevon Kearse had two in Wade Hummel and Hoover. Henry had two in Hampton and Lee Peters.

Henry did not stand out with the first impression he made on Hampton, a gritty, short man of the South who had knots in his stomach before regular-season games, loved working with defensive backs, and relished taking road trips so that he could eat at his favorite restaurant, Steak 'n Shake.

"I wasn't paying a whole lot of attention to him," Hampton said. "I never really thought to start looking at him until the second semester when I got him into weight class. I noticed his work ethic. He was a little quiet kid who didn't say much.

"As a sophomore, he was the quarterback of the jayvee team. It gave him some experience. We moved him up to varsity. And toward the end of the season, he was playing with us as a defensive back, just to get him some playing time. He had speed. You started working with him in the clinics and stuff like that. He could throw the ball. He was getting a little bit bigger and a little bit taller.

"I'd go up there to pick those kids up. He would always be sitting there by that little post. I'd pick him up in the summer for workouts. Anytime he had an off day when the buses weren't running, I'd go back and get him and take him home. It was a rough place. People would walk into their apartment and steal their stuff. They had to watch out for that. But the kids, they all hung together. He developed his own work ethic. He was self-motivated. He knew what he wanted to do."

Even after Henry became a multimillionaire NFL player, he took on Hampton's habit of searching garage sales for deals on furniture. When booking flights for Fort Myers, Henry always looked for the cheapest airfares.

"That's one of the main reasons I've been going in the direction I've been going," Henry said of Hampton. "That's one of the great relationships I've had throughout my whole life. It's one of the most important ones. He steered me in the right direction. He didn't have to. He didn't have to do anything that he did for me.

"He took me to Fellowship of Christian Athlete football camps and Bible studies. We still have a great relationship. He's like a second father to me. Same with Anthony Dixon. All of those guys."

Not until late in his college career at the University of South Florida did playing in the NFL even seem like a possibility to Henry. He wasn't even highly recruited, in part because he had poor standardized test scores. He had to sit out his freshman year of college because of them.

"You never knew what was going to transpire," Hampton said of Henry's college recruitment. "If he were being recruited today, he probably wouldn't have gotten looked at. If you have a great junior year, you're already offered a scholarship these days. These kids who come on strong as seniors, they get lost these days."

In 1996, the circumstances made Henry a perfect fit for the then-fledgling University of South Florida football program. Coach Jim Leavitt, hired to build the program from scratch, needed players, and he needed them fast. South Florida did not play games its first season. That allowed Henry to get his grades in order and learn the college system. At South Florida, Henry honed what Hampton taught him, playing for Leavitt and the late Andre Waters, who coached the defensive backs for the Bulls.

"I never dreamed of being a professional athlete," Henry said. "A lot of the guys who went to Estero did. I played football out in the neighborhood. And I loved basketball. That was the game I really loved to play. But I never dreamed of playing in the NFL. My college coach, Andre Waters, my junior year, he told me, 'I think you have what it takes to play at the next level.' That's when I started focusing on doing it. That's when I started focusing on training more."

Waters, who played ten of his twelve seasons in 1984–93 with the Philadelphia Eagles, had a Hampton-like impact on Henry.

"The best thing was that they had Andre Waters as their secondary coach," Hampton said. "He was teaching him everything. Anthony, he was eating it up. In all that time, he just did his thing."

Waters, also a cornerback and also a Florida native, grew up in the impoverished community of Belle Glade, two hours east of Fort Myers and the birth city of Jevon Kearse's father. Waters related well to Henry, all the while suffering from post-concussion syndrome. On November 20, 2006, Waters shot himself to death at his Tampa home. He was forty-four, but an autopsy revealed a brain that looked closer to eighty-five years old.

"That was devastating to Anthony," Hampton said of Waters's suicide. "That just broke his heart. Andre called him the night before. Anthony couldn't get back to him or something. Then he got the call the next morning. Anthony was just devastated."

Henry had the same agent Waters had, Philadelphia-based Jerrold Colton.

"It's hard for me to talk about it, because Andre was one of my closest friends," Colton said when asked about Waters's impact on Henry. "They had a tremendous coach-player relationship that was also like a father-son relationship, and as close friends.

"Andre was a kid from a small town, too. He couldn't run. He wasn't big. He had a twelve-year career in the NFL. Anthony was a far, far better athlete. Andre was a tremendous teacher for Anthony. He taught him how to play the game at a higher level. If it had been another coach, I don't know if Anthony would have realized how good he was."

Because Henry always aspired to improve as a player, he never considered the rising opinions that he could play as well as anyone in the NFL.

"I remember it was coming up on his senior year," Hampton said. "Now the dilemma is, if he graduated within four years, the NCAA would grant him another year of eligibility, because he had to sit out as a freshman.

"So in the spring, he takes about twenty-some hours of credits. He had boxes of energy bars, because he was always having to eat on the run, going from classes to practice."

Henry achieved that degree, using the extra year of eligibility to his advantage. After Henry's senior season at South Florida, Henry applied for a job with an NFL team, but he wasn't applying to be a player.

"I was looking to do an internship with the Bucs in community relations," Henry said. "I got my degree in communications. I went and interviewed. They said that they wanted me to come back and do a second interview. When I got that, that's when I got the invitation to go to the NFL Combine."

Colton laughed when he remembered that.

"It's an ironic thing, because he was applying for a job with the Tampa Bay Buccaneers, and they were one of the teams interested in drafting him as a player," Colton said. "I'll tell you when I first fell in love with him as a player. The Super Bowl was in Tampa that year [2001]. I came down, and I saw Anthony do some agility drills. When I saw Anthony do the 'L' drill, I knew he was special."

In the L drill, also known as the three-cone drill, an athlete arranges the cones into a triangle with five yards in between each one.

The athlete then sprints an L-shaped pattern between the cones. Just thinking about it could tire an NFL cornerback, but not Henry.

"It shows what kind of hips and feet he has, which is the key to being a corner," Colton said. "All you had to do was be around him and see his seriousness. He's an extremely, extremely bright man. You see how grounded he is. I really believe he's as good as it gets in so many ways.

"It's as rewarding a relationship as I've ever had. He's one of the finest people I've ever known. I've never seen or heard of Anthony doing anything that you wouldn't want your father or your son to do. He's just a true role model."

Henry took little time showing he belonged on an NFL team and not in a team's community relations department. The Cleveland Browns selected Henry in the fourth round of the 2001 NFL Draft with the ninety-seventh overall pick.

"I remember on the day of the draft, he was a 'riser' on Mel Kiper's list," Colton said. "When ESPN flashed their best player available on the screen, he was on there for a while. He was a little disappointed in not getting taken on the first day."

On September 23, 2001, Henry tied a Cleveland Browns record for interceptions in a game by picking off three passes against the Detroit Lions. Henry returned the second interception 58 yards before finally getting shoved out of bounds. He finished his rookie season with 10 interceptions, tied for the single-season franchise record. Only nine other NFL players since 1985 had snagged that many picks in one season. Henry also became the first Cleveland player to pick off three passes in two different games the same season.

"I was supposed to be a backup," Henry said. "But then some guys got hurt. Then I would come in on passing downs. I would come in, and I was just blessed to make plays. I couldn't have even dreamed it that way. It's one thing to not even think about being in the NFL to actually being in the NFL and leading the league in interceptions the first year."

Estero High School retired Henry's jersey number 3 on May 5, 2004. The school named its awards for its male and female athletes of the year the Anthony Henry Outstanding Athlete Awards.

"It's a big deal for me," Henry said. "I never thought I would get to the point where I had a jersey retired. It's a blessing for me to have something like that happen. My family, Coach Hampton, and everybody I played ball with have to share some of the credit. It's not just an honor for myself, but for everyone I ever played with."

In 2005, Henry signed a five-year, $25 million deal with the Dallas Cowboys, with $12 million being guaranteed.

"He had always wanted to get a BMW," Colton said. "He called me up not long after signing that contract, and he asked me if it would be alright to get one now. I said, 'Anthony, you're a grown man. That's your money. You can do whatever you want to with it.'"

Said Hampton: "He stayed grounded. A lot of those other players, when they get all of that money, they don't know how to handle it. They spend like crazy. They end up with four or five cars. A lot of them are broke."

In 2007, Henry ranked second on the Cowboys with 81 tackles, including a team-high 73 solos under Coach Bill Parcells. Henry had another fast start that season, picking off four passes—two in two games.

After four seasons with the Cleveland Browns, four with the Cowboys, and one with the Detroit Lions, Henry hit the home stretch on his career. The six-foot-one Henry entered the NFL at 205 pounds. Nine years later, the Lions listed him at 207.

"I never thought I would play at the professional level," Henry said. "Not because I wasn't good enough. I just thought that wasn't my main focus. I saw Deion Sanders play in the NFL, but I never thought I would play in the NFL. In hindsight, it worked out better for me that way. You look at some young guys today, and that's their only focus."

Just as Henry found success coming out of the Michigan Court housing projects, so did one of his childhood roommates. The family of Earnest Graham took in Henry and his family for a few months in the 1980s. Alto Henry Sr. and Graham's stepfather were brothers.

Graham went on to have a much higher-profile high school football career than Henry, but he also endured a much tougher road to NFL riches.

 **Being Earnest**

The little boy stood at the top of the second-story windowsill. His single-parent mother, Sandra Smith, worked three jobs at the time in order to support her four children, entrusting her two youngest sons' care to a babysitter during many a sweltering summer afternoon.

They lived in a two-bedroom apartment in the Michigan Court housing projects. Built for people living through hard times, the two-story apartments served as homes to many with low incomes but high hopes for escaping the monotony of the small-city ghetto.

The boy, seven years old, looked down from the window at a childhood friend one story below, beckoning him to jump.

Some friend.

The ensuing plummet resulted in a sprained ankle. It would not be the last such injury Earnest Graham would suffer.

"When I found out, I said, 'If he's not hurt, I'm going to beat his butt,'" Sandra Smith said with a laugh, recalling the incident, which happened a couple of years after her son descended to the ground floor in a different manner, riding down the stairs on a Big Wheel.

"He was not afraid of anything," she told me during one of many conversations I had with her prior to her death from cancer at age fifty-seven in 2010.

Graham's fearlessness would serve him well during his journey to the NFL as a running back. The journey almost didn't happen.

"E. G. is one of my favorite life-journey stories," said Tim Maloney, who coached Graham in basketball at Mariner High School in Cape Coral, where Graham teamed with high school All-American Teddy Dupay, helping to form one of the nation's best backcourts.

Born on January 15, 1980, Graham appeared destined for the NFL as a running back at Mariner, where he amassed a then–Lee County record of 5,710 rushing yards before moving on to the University of Florida.

Everyone had high expectations for Graham as a youth athlete. His absent father, Earnest Graham Sr., had excelled at football, making a name for himself as a prominent high school running back during the late 1960s at the all-black Dunbar High and then, following integration, at Cypress Lake High.

"He was awesome," said Tommy Battle of the elder Graham. Battle played quarterback on the 1968 Dunbar Tigers team, while Graham started at fullback.

"He was thick, big, and fast," Battle said. "He was a big back with a lot of speed. The longest touchdown of my career, I handed off to Earnest Graham. He broke tackles and ran 98 yards."

Graham Sr. may have been good at scoring touchdowns, but he did not score many points as a father to Earnest and Brandon Graham. Earnest Graham's older siblings, Shawn Pope, a prolific high school running back in his own right, and Alfreka Bloomfield, had different fathers but were raised in the same home with their mother.

"After high school, I ended up getting married and tried to be a married man," Graham Sr. said. "I'd probably go out Friday and Saturday all the time. And my wife, she didn't take to that too well."

A divorce ensued. So did more lapses in judgment.

"I eventually hung out with the dope guys," Graham said. That wasn't hard to do. They were everywhere in their neighborhood. "I spent my years being a doper or a junkie. I came out of that to being a preacher. It took me about three years to get away from the drugs completely and not fall back and forth into it."

Graham spent two years in prison in the mid-1980s for grand theft. Then he focused on his faith as a Christian.

"That was a good experience, because it let me see what I needed to do," Graham said of his time in prison. "It makes you appreciate being free. After that, it has been nothing but a life dedicated to ministry and preaching."

Graham lived in Mississippi for fifteen years. He said he preached at various churches there before moving back to Florida. His life as a renewed Christian still kept him from playing a role as a father, leaving Earnest Graham Jr. as the man of his house.

"I can count on my hands how many times I've seen him in the past ten or twelve years," Graham Jr. told the *News-Press* while in college. "But we're on good terms."

Graham Jr. was made aware of his father's playing days while at Mariner.

"They always said I'd never be as good as he was," Graham said. "I figured he was a good athlete back in the day. I had heard stories from my mom and uncle."

When Graham Sr. finally watched his namesake play a game at Mariner, he walked out of the stands knowing his son played football better than he ever could. "When I first started reading about him, I wondered if the other team was that bad or if he was that good," Graham Sr. said. "So when I went to see him, I realized. I could hardly believe he could move that fast once he got his hands on the ball. He's so powerful. When I see Earnest, I see a prayer answered from God to me."

The Odd Couple

Earnest Graham Jr. answered the prayers of many Mariner High sports fans in 1995–98, as did Teddy Dupay. Never had two such awesome athletes played to their full potential on a nationally recognized level at the same time and at the same school in Southwest Florida.

Dupay never played football, but he teamed with Graham on the basketball court and on the baseball diamond. Dupay and Graham forever remain linked in Mariner lore because of their closeness as friends, their elite skills in multiple sports, and their choosing the University of Florida.

After Graham set county records on the football field, Dupay, a five-foot, ten-inch, 170-pound guard, set local, state, and numerous tournament records across the country on the basketball court.

Dupay, who is white, averaged 41.5 points per game as a senior. He scored a career-high 70 points during a playoff game against Miami Cooper City. Many of the Cooper City players posed for photographs and asked for Dupay's autograph following their 112–89 loss. Dupay obliged. He had made 20 of 40 field goals in that game, including 13 of 26 from behind the 3-point line. He also made 17 of 19 free throws. Graham wasn't exactly a spectator in that game, either. He chipped in with 19 points.

Graham had a pretty good vantage point to witness almost all of Dupay's career record 3,744 points, which topped the state scoring record held by Chris Corchiani, who played at North Carolina State and briefly in the NBA. "We kicked butt," Dupay said. "We set records. We set records in basketball in Southwest Florida that will never be set again. We had a great run."

Graham and Dupay had comparable statistics in baseball. As juniors, Dupay hit .477 with 26 stolen bases. Graham hit .379 with 21 stolen bases. As a senior, Dupay hit .371 with 2 home runs and posted a 7–0 record for Mariner's tennis team. Graham hit .328 with 5 home runs and 9 stolen bases.

As they matured, moving from being the big fish in a small pond to the University of Florida's nationally ranked football and basketball programs, they found different circles of friends. Dupay ended up tarnishing his tenure on the Florida basketball team when Gators coach Billy Donovan dismissed him from the program his junior year because of gambling allegations.

"As far as my career, it was more about the bad decisions I made," said Dupay, who insisted he did not provide gamblers with inside information from the Florida basketball team. He cited gambling on the 2001 Super Bowl between the Baltimore Ravens and New York Giants as one of the mistakes that got him in trouble.

"What I was accused of was helping people who gambled on campus," Dupay said. "Some of those people were my friends. At the end of the day, I was friends with people who were gambling. None of that had anything to do with Florida basketball. Of course I wonder what would have happened. Not getting to play my senior year . . . it still hurts me to this day. My senior year, I was healthy, I was ready to go. To this day, looking back, I don't feel the penalty fit the crime. But it doesn't matter. I'm OK with that now. It's taken me a long time to get a grip on that."

Instead of being able to pad his basketball resumé and prepare for the 2002 NBA Draft, Dupay plodded through professional basketball's underworld, playing out of the country in Venezuela and in the country for Phoenix in the American Basketball Association.

Dupay, the son of an affluent two-parent family with an orthopedic surgeon for a father, fell fast from his athletic grace. Graham, the son of an absent father and a hardworking mother, kept climbing.

"Earnest is one of the best success stories in the NFL, not just because of what he went through his first couple of years," Dupay said. "Take a look at anybody who has played eight years in the NFL. People who play eight years in the NFL, I would say less than 10 percent of them are undrafted free agents. How many guys in the NFL for nine years didn't get drafted? Not very many."

Even back in the eighth grade, Dupay thought of Earnest Graham as someone destined for success. "He was very wise," Dupay said. "He was the smartest guy in our group. He processed information different from the rest of us."

Listed at five feet, nine inches and 225 pounds, Graham by no means had an easy path to the pros. As Graham ascended the rocky road that would lead him to NFL riches, his younger brother Brandon descended into the drug underworld of Fort Myers, choosing the wrong way out of Dunbar.

Struggle Builds Character

Earnest Graham Jr. and Brandon Graham have tattoos that say "Struggle Builds Character" on their forearms. They played running back at Mariner. They are the children of Sandra Smith and Earnest Graham Sr.

Their similarities, for the most part, end there.

While Earnest Graham Jr. avoided his father's missteps, Brandon Graham did not. While Earnest Graham emulated the forward running style of Emmitt Smith, Brandon Graham tried and failed to be like Barry Sanders, often getting tackled behind the line of scrimmage.

Earnest Graham almost always moved forward upon getting the ball in his hands. Brandon Graham, two years younger than Earnest, would either get an 8-yard gain or an 8-yard loss, trying to make things happen. He lost too much ground off the field as well. His trouble began with being in the wrong place at the wrong time at the age of sixteen, when he was present at the nonfatal shooting in the leg of a rival football player, Fort Myers High School's Danny McGee, in 1998.

"That should have been a wake-up call," said Mike Vogt, who coached Earnest and Brandon at Mariner before moving on to Florida's Space Coast near Melbourne. "There's a term called slippage. I learned it from a basketball coach, and I use it all the time. The point is, when you don't have control of a situation, that is when kids have to make choices on their own. And there's nothing you can do about it."

Brandon Graham's legal problems escalated. They became routine. He would get caught doing something, get a warning, and then move on to the next step in illegal behavior. It all culminated on February 2, 2007, when police arrested Brandon and charged him with conspiracy to distribute more than 50 grams of crack cocaine. Police found 721 grams of marijuana, 96 grams of crack cocaine, 11 grams of powder cocaine, two handguns, ammunition, and $1,500 in cash. Police estimated the drugs to have a street value of about $14,000.

"A lot of times, I had minor brushes with the police," Brandon said. "It was kind of a slap on the hand. As years went by, I got smarter and better at what I was doing."

Brandon's luck at committing crimes eventually ran out. He described his next home, the Lee County Jail, as "the worst place on Earth." He pleaded guilty in May 2007, receiving a seventy-month prison sentence.

Just before Brandon Graham's sentencing, Earnest Graham wrote a letter to the judge. He made no mention in it of his occupation as a Tampa Bay Buccaneers running back. He urged the judge not to give his little brother a lenient sentence, asking the judge to give Brandon enough time in prison to rehabilitate himself.

"Honestly, my brother has escaped a lot of troubles," Earnest Graham wrote. "In today's world, it's sad to say, but people were drawn to him because of this, and I think my brother misjudged the attention he was receiving. As his brother, I do have to say I am hoping that the courts give him enough time to learn his lesson, nothing more, nothing less. He is ready to change, and I can tell that he has already started the process."

That process of Brandon Graham rehabilitating himself wasn't pretty. Sentenced to the Coleman Federal Correctional Complex, the same place that housed Ronnie Tape, Brandon Graham had to make some serious adjustments to the prison lifestyle. Rolled bands of steel barbed wire—too many to count—and multiple concrete walls, barriers, and guarded gates separated Brandon and about 1,700 other Coleman inmates from the lush northern Florida countryside and their freedom. Inside, he came to know Tape, as they shared the same musical aspirations.

Earnest Graham, Sandra Smith, and many others had pleaded with Brandon over the years to remove himself from the culture of lawlessness, to steer clear of the path set years before him by Tape. Instead, Brandon ended up in prison with him.

"It wasn't that I didn't listen," Brandon Graham told the *News-Press* during his prison sentence. "I was going down my own road. I knew what this type of life would bring, because I've seen so many people go through it. But sometimes you have to go through something in life in order to understand it. If I weren't here today, I'd probably be doing the same stupid stuff."

During Earnest Graham's breakout 2007 NFL season, he visited Brandon almost weekly. They would talk for an hour or two at a time, going over Brandon's desire to become a music producer or a sports bar owner. They talked about Brandon's goal of helping Earnest with his charity foundation, Earnest Giving, Inc., and they discussed how Earnest fulfilled some of Brandon's dreams by emerging as the starting tailback for the Buccaneers. Brandon told Earnest where he wanted his first post-prison meal: Red Lobster.

"A lot of people think that I'm upset because it's not me," Brandon said of his brother becoming an NFL running back and millionaire. "When it's game day, it's my game day. I'm actually living my pro dreams through him. He had to go through a lot. We both had to struggle, but that has built us into the people we are today."

The brothers were different on the football field and off it as well, and that went beyond Brandon's penchant for putting himself into trouble.

"Earnest was a better student," former Mariner coach Vogt said. Earnest earned the 1998 Rotary South Scholar Athlete of the Year Award, given to Lee County's best achiever. "He had his priorities a lot better off. But Brandon was a young kid. A lot of kids grow out of that. One-on-one and work ethic and ability, they were very comparable. It was when the bag was out from underneath the porch and you had no control of it when there were differences. Honestly, I really liked Brandon. He had a lot of personality. He was a likeable kid. He's really intelligent. He's not a kid who can't think and can't read and can't write. He's got a strong mind behind him."

Michael McNerney, the principal during the time that all of Sandra Smith's children attended Mariner, noticed the same character traits in Brandon and Earnest.

"Earnest was an extremely focused individual," McNerney said. "It was more personal with Earnest. It was pretty evident that he had his goals in mind, all along. He knew where the finish line was. Brandon was always searching, always searching for where the finish line was."

Like Sandra Smith, Vogt had no answer for why Earnest took one path and Brandon another.

"If I had an answer for it, I wouldn't be coaching anymore," Vogt said. "I'd be on TV and making millions of dollars."

Understanding why Earnest Graham took the path to making millions in the NFL while Brandon Graham spent almost five years of his life in prison wasn't hard to figure out after the brothers had time to reflect.

"It all comes down to influences," Earnest Graham said. He wore a pair of long, black shorts and a sleeveless, gray T-shirt, his biceps bulging. He leaned over a bowl of gumbo, eating it with a fork at Lee Roy Selmon's off Daniels Parkway in Fort Myers, a restaurant named for and once partly owned by the late Tampa Bay Buccaneers Hall of Fame defensive end. "I have very few friends who have done illegal things," Earnest Graham said.

That wasn't the case with Brandon.

"I'm into the rap thing," said Brandon, who, as Earnest spoke from the relaxing setting of the restaurant, sat in the confines of his prison cell, eating prison food. "Now, I realize that these rappers are just entertainers. But those young kids think that rappers are a way of life. They take what rappers are saying, and they live it as everyday life. Some rappers glorify the wrong things. I don't want to say that rappers are wrong. At the end of the day, they are supporting their families."

Although Earnest Graham listened to the same music, he differentiated the fantasy from the reality when Brandon did not.

"I never was attracted to the street life," Earnest Graham said. "I just loved sports. And I was in love with music. I was always a think-first person. If I do this, this is what happens."

In Dunbar, Brandon Graham said, the children have few, if any, role models other than the drug dealers.

"The kids don't have anything or anybody to look up to except for what they see," Brandon Graham said of the kids in his old neighborhood. "And all they see are drugs. Everyone I looked up to is in here with me. The people I followed, I'm in here with them. In this game, you're never going to win. I want to believe that a kid will read this, and that he will change. In my heart, I know he won't, because he will have to come and see it from this point of view. Once I got here, it opened my eyes."

Sandra Smith had higher hopes.

"I just hope this will help someone out there," Smith said of telling the story of Earnest and Brandon. "There's just a certain line you can't cross over, and getting back home is hell. I miss my baby. I can't even begin to describe how much my heart hurts. Our family is here to support him with the journey back home."

In 2009, Sandra Smith was diagnosed with cancer. She endured chemotherapy treatments as she monitored her youngest son's rehabilitation in prison.

In October 2010, Brandon Graham finally got released from prison into a halfway house. The next month, on November 7, Sandra Smith succumbed to cancer. She lived long enough to see her youngest son reclaim his freedom and long enough to see her second-youngest son transform himself into Florida's Mr. Football, a high school All-American, one of the best backs in University of Florida history and then an NFL starter, all the while overcoming any and every challenge sent his way.

Making a Name

Earnest Graham once caught, threw, and rushed for a touchdown during the same game for the Mariner Tritons. He did that as a high school freshman. A starter on the most talented basketball team in Southwest Florida history, Graham possibly could have been a Division I player in that sport as well. Graham also excelled at baseball. The Philadelphia Phillies drafted him in the forty-third round of the 1998 draft, making him the 1,273rd overall pick. As more and more athletes began specializing in certain sports, Graham finished his Mariner tenure as one of Southwest Florida's last great three-sport stars.

"I thought it was a mistake that I didn't play baseball," Graham said, four years into his NFL career. "And I still do. The Philadelphia Phillies had talked to me. They had two No. 1 picks that year, and they told me they would take me with their second No. 1 pick if I gave up football. I decided I would go to school instead."

Graham's fame and legend as a prep player grew as he progressed through Mariner. He rushed for 2,159 yards and 33 touchdowns as a junior. He missed two games because of an injury as a senior, but he still rushed for 1,858 yards and 29 touchdowns, winning Florida's Class 5A Mr. Football award.

At the University of Florida, Graham played for a throw-first coach in Steve Spurrier. Graham still managed to finish as the fifth all-time leading rusher in program history with 3,065 yards.

Poor performances as an NFL prospect in the 40-yard dash and an injury at the time of the NFL Scouting Combine meant Graham would go undrafted and overlooked as a prospect except for the team closest to his home, the Tampa Bay Buccaneers.

The Buccaneers, then coached by Jon Gruden, invited Graham to training camp in 2003 before giving him an injury settlement and re-leasing him. Earnest's wife, Alicia, gave birth to their daughter, Aiyana, on March 23, 2003. They spent the following spring moving in and out of cheap hotels in Tampa, as their funds from the injury settlement and the lack of a pro contract had evaporated.

"It was all so uncertain at that time," said Alicia Graham, a Fort My-ers native and a Fort Myers High School graduate. "He was doing so well before the injury. The good thing was that they gave him a settle-ment. They let him know they would be taking a look at him."

Graham landed with the Cleveland Browns' eight-man practice squad for a week late during the 2003 season, but the Browns released him on November 26.

"It was in '04 that we couldn't afford to live there anymore," Alicia said of their apartment. Then they ended up sharing an apartment with four men. Alicia and Earnest Graham never gave up on his professional football career.

"You could always see the silver lining," she said. "I knew how hard he worked at it. There was never a time when I said, 'Honey, you need to give this up.' It was never like that. Earnest is always going to do his job. He's going to be prepared. He's going to be focused."

Graham finally caught on with the Buccaneers in 2004. He earned the nickname Mr. August for leading the team in preseason rushing yardage three years in a row. That production came in handy during the 2007 season, when first-round draft pick and starting tailback Carnell "Cadillac" Williams went down with a season-ending knee injury.

Even before Williams went down, Gruden openly wondered whether Graham might be the best back on his team. Graham answered that question. In 2007, he became the first back in franchise history to rush for touchdowns in six consecutive games. His 10 rushing touchdowns were the third-highest single-season total in franchise history. Heading into that 2008 season, Graham hired Drew Rosenhaus as his agent. Rosenhaus negotiated with the Buccaneers, who rewarded Graham with a contract that would set him up for the rest of his life: a four-year deal worth $11.05 million.

The Graham family, who by then had welcomed son Earnest Myles to the world, upgraded from their modest, three-bedroom home. In 2009, the Grahams paid $545,000 for a four-bedroom home in Lutz, just north of Tampa. The home had almost two acres of land, and it had fallen in price from more than $800,000 during the economic recession and real estate crash. The Grahams also purchased a fleet of twenty trucks and started a trucking company while preparing for life after football.

"When he's done playing, we don't want to worry about how to afford our lifestyle," Alicia Graham said during the final days of her husband's playing career. "We aren't going to have a lot of the financial issues that a lot of ex-athletes have."

While planning for the future, which included co-owning an insurance company with Cadillac Williams, Earnest Graham relished the chance to make an impact in the present.

On November 4, 2007, Graham ran out of the Raymond James Stadium tunnel and started in front of more than sixty-five thousand fans. He rushed for 124 yards and a touchdown for his first 100-yard game in an NFL uniform as Tampa Bay defeated the Arizona Cardinals 17–10.

"Coming from where I came from to going to the University of Florida—I didn't think I'd ever get to do that," Graham said after that game. "But once good things start to happen, it can definitely happen to you.

"For anybody out there who's in the situation that I was in—if they keep working hard, they'll ultimately get the chance. I always tried to keep my eyes on the prize. I always wanted to be better."

Breaking Through

Earnest Graham made about $600,000 in 2007 and entered that season as primarily a special teams player. His duties included blocking for Tampa Bay's kick returner, trying to tackle the opposing team's returner, and, on occasion, receiving a carry at tailback or making a block at fullback.

In order to make a leap from earning a half million to a million dollars, Graham needed to make a comparable leap on the field, and he needed more playing time after the August exhibition season ended.

"That never bothered me," Graham said of his Mr. August nickname. "That's probably why I've been in the league so long."

Prior to 2007, Graham had rushed 52 times for 215 yards and caught 1 pass for 4 yards in his first three NFL seasons. The numbers were far from spectacular, but more and more, Gruden liked what he saw.

Even before starter and 2005 first-round draft pick Cadillac Williams suffered his season-ending knee injury in 2007, Gruden intended to give Graham more playing time. That preseason, Gruden gave Graham his fewest number of preseason carries, typically a sign that he wanted to preserve him for the regular season. Graham's patience paid off. One week before Williams went down for the season, Graham broke out on September 23 for a then–career high of 75 rushing yards and his first 2 NFL touchdowns on just 8 carries against the St. Louis Rams. His days as an exclusive special teams player had ended.

"Oh, man," an exasperated teammate and linebacker Barrett Ruud said after that game. "No more Mr. August. He's Mr. September, October, November, December now. He's a great player. He's one of the better players on this team, to be honest with you."

On his first professional football touchdown, Graham, with legs pumping and shoulders lowered, bounced off defenders and his own offensive linemen for an 8-yard score and a 17-3 lead. Later, he burst up the middle for a 28-yard touchdown, stiff-arming a defender five yards from the end zone during the fourth quarter and then shoving his way in for the score.

"Obviously, Earnest exploded onto the scene," Gruden said that day. "And the big question is, why in the heck hasn't he been playing? Obviously, now we have to put our minds together and figure out how to get Earnest more involved, because clearly he's also deserving of the football. And that's a good problem to have."

For the rest of 2007, Graham gave opposing defenses plenty of problems, finishing with 898 rushing yards and 10 touchdowns. That tied James Wilder and Mike Alstott for the third-highest single-season total for rushing touchdowns, trailing Wilder's 13 in 1984 and Errict Rhett's 11 in 1995.

Earnest Graham jerseys were not being manufactured from 2003 through the start of 2007. But by the end of 2007, they were being made and selling out. By November, Graham had filmed a commercial for a Chrysler Jeep Dodge dealership in Tampa, the first such endorsement opportunity for him. On June 30, 2008, Graham signed a three-year, $10.5 million contract extension.

"Things have changed," Graham said. "I haven't changed."

Accolades for Earnest

Soon after wealth and fame arrived for Graham, the City of Fort Myers renamed a street Earnest Graham Avenue in his honor. Lisa Martin, who lived on Graham Avenue, petitioned the city to add Earnest's first name to the street name.

"Earnest Graham, his story is quite fascinating," said Martin, the mother of four and a die-hard Bucs fan. "He's a true Cinderella story. Kids look up to somebody like him. He's a great kid. He was raised by a single mother. Not all of those kids make it. I was a single mom for many years. There's a lot that can come out of his story."

Other awards and honors came Graham's way.

Mariner High invited him back in order to retire his number 5 football jersey.

The following summer, the Fort Myers Miracle, the Class A affiliate of the Minnesota Twins, invited Graham to throw out the ceremonial first pitch before playing the St. Lucie Mets.

Graham brought his family to the game, and Mariner baseball coach Steve Larsen also attended. "It was fun for him," Larsen said of Graham playing high school baseball. "With Earnest, he went from football to basketball and then to baseball. There wasn't a whole lot of pressure on him like in the other two sports. It seemed like he was relaxed, and his true athletic ability was able to show. He had a lot of power. And he was a great teammate. His first love was football. He loved football first. I'm not one to question what he loves to do."

There was something else that Larsen did not question: that if Graham had devoted himself to baseball year-round like the country's other elite prospects, he would have played in the major leagues.

"Without a doubt," Larsen said.

Father Knows Best

If Earnest Graham wasn't off bowling with Cadillac Williams during his spare time, he would be with his wife, Alicia, and their two children, daughter Aiyana and son Earnest Myles.

"Earnest Myles has changed his life," said Sandra Smith, whose own life was transformed upon becoming a grandmother. "He's all boy. All boy. There's a new sheriff in town."

Alicia Graham said her husband had talked about having five or six kids. That talk died down when Earnest Myles learned to walk at nine months old.

"It's the most challenging thing I've ever done in my life," Earnest said of being a father. "It's just challenging. You have to teach them about the world. You want them to be smart and intelligent. You try to get them prepared for what they are going to face.

"That's my biggest fear. You don't want them to have any pain in their life. But you know they'll have to go through it in order to grow up."

Earnest Graham, like so many children around him in that Michigan Court housing project, rarely saw his father. Although he had the influence of his uncles and the legacy of his grandfather—Louis Carter was the first black pharmacist in Fort Myers—Graham became the man of the house at an early age.

"It amazes me to know that I have a son of Earnest's character," Earnest Graham Sr. said. "I know he didn't get it from me. If he got it from anyone, he got it from his mom."

As an adult and as a father, Graham the son pledged to break the cycle of single-parenthood.

"It happens a lot, because growing up, what you see is what you remember," Earnest Graham said of fathers deserting their children. "My mother instilled in me responsibility. She instilled in me to be a good father. She taught me that it was something to look forward to."

Said Sandra Smith: "That's what makes me so proud of him."

As an adult, Earnest Graham would see his father more often, but he maintained a relationship with him at a guarded distance. When the Fort Myers Miracle baseball team honored Graham, inviting him to throw a game's ceremonial first pitch and dubbing it "Earnest Graham Day," Earnest Graham Sr. attended the game and cheered on his son.

"He obviously wasn't ready [to be a father]," Earnest Graham said of his father's demeanor, years ago. "It just made me learn things on my own. My mom did a pretty good job of showing me how to see things in the world."

Graham Sr. said his biggest regret was not being a role model as a father.

"I think about my father and my mother after they divorced," Graham Sr. said. "I didn't keep in touch with my father. We didn't keep in close contact. Maybe that's a part of the Graham character. When I see Earnest, I go see him, and everything is fine. We talk and laugh and hug. But we never really sit down and talk about things that are important. There's a lot of things that I think I can share with him—things you have to face in college. But I never had that kind of relationship with him. That bothers me pretty much more than anything."

Alicia Graham remains thankful that her children will have a more complete upbringing than her husband did.

"His children are what drive him," Alicia Graham said. "They inspire him. He always takes them down to the locker room and carries them around there. He takes so much inspiration from his children. He'll play with them all day. He's always thinking of something for them to do."

"This whole experience?" Sandra Smith said, of watching her children and grandchildren grow. "They have taken my breath away, they really have. It's just been a blessing."

13 Revelation in Atlanta

Five men stormed through the door of Phillip Buchanon's Atlanta condominium.

They wore ski masks. They carried guns. They meant business.

At 3:00 a.m. on March 13, 2006, before the gunmen arrived, Buchanon's life already was flashing before him. The five-foot, eleven-inch, 186-pound NFL cornerback, about to enter his second season with the Houston Texans after falling out with the Oakland Raiders, was sitting on a leather couch, reminiscing with a former teammate about their days at Lehigh Senior High School, just east of Fort Myers. They were talking about their coach, Larry Gary. They were talking about their team, which featured five Division I college prospects. They were talking about missed opportunities, about how the 1998 Lehigh Lightning failed in their quest for a state playoff berth, let alone winning a state championship. They were talking about the good old days, which at times really weren't so good.

Born on September 19, 1980, eleven years after integration came to Fort Myers, Buchanon did not have a father in the home. His father, James Buchanon, worked as a teacher for the Lee County School

District, later in his life becoming an assistant high school principal, a rare position of leadership for a local black man. He did not stay with Phillip's mom for long, and he went on to have three other children, Phillip's half siblings.

Phillip and James Buchanon never were that close.

Asked to name the father figure in his life, Phillip Buchanon paused long. He credited Coach Gary, but Buchanon also credited himself. Buchanon ran the 40-yard dash in 4.3 seconds. He became one of the most highly recruited cornerbacks from Dunbar since Deion Sanders, almost fifteen years after Sanders graduated from North Fort Myers High School. No father figure, Buchanon said, could have put him on that path any better than he did himself.

Phillip's mother, Anne Davis, had her hands full while raising him. She would have six children after Phillip: Harry, Nicole, Jeremy, Malia, Tyree, and E. J. They lived for most of Buchanon's childhood on Bert Drive, eight blocks east of Deion Sanders's childhood home. Buchanon, however, roved among the homes of friends and family members.

"I grew up pretty much all over Fort Myers," Buchanon said. "I spent a lot of time in Sabal Palms. I could have been in the Old Projects. I could have been in the New Projects. Describe Sabal Palms? You have different types of backgrounds there. You have houses there with moms and dads living there. It's kind of more stable. Then you have the apartments. That's mostly single moms and the kids living there. We had fun there.

"There was always something going on at Sabal Palms. It was like a big playground for me. There would be fights. We would be playing football. We'd hang out there. I spent more time at Sabal Palms than at home growing up.

"My mom's house was really in the middle. I would go from my grandma's house to my mom's house, but on the way there, I'd stop at Sabal Palms. I would walk everywhere. When I was growing up, I used to walk from Michigan Avenue all the way to the Edison Mall."

That would be an almost five-mile walk each way.

"At the same time though, as we walked, there were peoples' houses on the way that we'd stop at," Buchanon said. "We moved a lot. We were poor, but we weren't poor to the point where we couldn't eat or anything like that. But at the same time, we didn't have the best situation, either. There was a lot of stuff going on that wasn't right. That's one of the things you have to deal with when you're growing up in an urban neighborhood."

Buchanon took an active role in following the athletic career of his brother Jeremy Davis, who, eleven years younger than him, evolved into a standout running back and cornerback at Fort Myers and Cape Coral High Schools. Davis accepted a scholarship in 2010 to play where Phillip did, at the University of Miami. Not qualified academically, Davis ended up going to prep school for a year before surfacing at the University of Central Florida.

A full generation, twenty-five years, separated Phillip Buchanon from his youngest brother, E. J. When E. J. was born in 2005, Phillip already was playing for his second NFL team and long since had left the house. He had moved out at age seventeen during his junior year of high school.

Growing up in Dunbar, Buchanon often received money, new clothes, and advice from drug dealers outside on the streets. Some of Buchanon's cousins once broke into his bedroom and stole his watch, his TV, and some shoes. Not long after the theft, Buchanon left. He moved into the home of Lehigh Senior High School teammate Nick Monsanto, who lived near the school located a solid twenty-minute drive east of Bert Drive. The crime wave had yet to seep into Lehigh Acres, a city that provided a haven for those who wanted to escape from urban Fort Myers into new, affordable homes. Buchanon still kept his ties to Dunbar. He had other help from people besides the Monsanto family, and Buchanon continued accepting financial support from neighborhood drug dealers.

"They took care of me," Buchanon said. They wanted him to succeed in athletics and urged him to avoid a life of crime. They may or may not have expected anything in return.

"They definitely respect you," said Buchanon, who is a cousin of fellow NFL player Jevon Kearse. "That's how it was when I was growing up. They tried to take care of certain kids."

As a child, Phillip had little to look forward to other than taking those crosstown walks to the Edison Mall, playing youth football, or playing basketball on the Sabal Palm courts with iron backboards, iron rims, and ragged or no nets.

By the age of ten, Phillip Buchanon had the self-confidence and awareness to realize he, like Deion Sanders, could leave Dunbar behind him. From afar, Buchanon admired Bo Jackson, an Alabama native who played baseball for the Kansas City Royals and football for the Oakland Raiders. At home, Buchanon idolized Fort Myers High's Jammi German, who some believed to be a more explosive high school football player than Sanders.

"I was a big Jammi German fan," Buchanon said. "At one point in time, I looked at Jammi German as the best player who ever came out of Fort Myers. He was definitely the guy."

Buchanon could do something better than even Jammi German could. He could hit a baseball. As a sophomore at Lehigh, Buchanon hit .400. That fell 100 points short of his goal of .500. In an era when African-American children were dropping baseball gloves in favor of basketballs and footballs, Buchanon and Earnest Graham were rare in that they continued to play hardball. While athletes both black and white began to specialize in specific sports, Buchanon excelled in four of them: football, basketball, baseball, and, when his baseball games did not conflict with meets, track and field.

By his senior year, Buchanon could cover the distance from second base to home plate—the 60-yard dash—faster than just about anyone. The Cincinnati Reds, a team that once employed Sanders, offered Buchanon a $500,000 signing bonus out of high school.

If you had grown up in near-poverty, if you had no real home anymore, if you had always wanted big-time money, you probably would have taken the money. I know I would have. For Buchanon, a half million dollars wasn't enough for him to give up his NFL aspirations. The money was never enough.

"If the price had been right, he might have taken it," Larry Gary said. "But I think his heart was always set on going to Miami and going to the NFL. As you know, most kids coming out of high school are going to take half a million dollars."

Something more than money motivated Buchanon. He wanted to be the best. In the summer between his junior and senior years at Lehigh, Buchanon attended the Nike football camp held in Coral Gables, Florida. Future NFL stars comprised the bulk of that camp's field: Andre Johnson, Antonio Bryant, Clinton Portis, Vernon Carey. They were all there. They would play in Pro Bowls. They would make millions of dollars. Back then, though, they were just rising high school seniors, and Buchanon fit right in. Buchanon shut down some of them, confirming what he had believed all along: he belonged.

"When I came back from that Nike camp, I knew what my opportunities were going to be," Buchanon said. "It was a solid turning point. Even though I had a lot of confidence in myself, I was even more confident when I came back from that. That's kind of how I view that."

Although Buchanon possessed some of Deion Sanders's cornerback skills, he did not have the same kind of charisma or ability to connect with the media. As a rookie with the Oakland Raiders, Buchanon called himself "Showtime" and spoke of himself in the third person. While Sanders could pull off such an act, Buchanon could not. The Oakland media just didn't get it, Buchanon said. The media helped promote the Deion Sanders Prime Time persona, but Buchanon did not get the same treatment as his boyhood hero. Buchanon's moodiness at the time did not endear him to his coaches in Oakland and especially in Houston, where Coach Gary Kubiak and Buchanon once engaged in a shouting match on the sidelines during a game.

"I was doomed from the start there," Buchanon said.

As 2005 turned to the off-season in 2006, Buchanon retreated to his condominium in Atlanta—he had another one in Miami—to have fun with his friends. Atlanta served as a playground for many off-season NFL athletes, many of whom lived in the city that closely reflected the NFL's racial demographics. Black players made up 65 percent of the NFL. Black residents made up 62 percent of Atlanta.

The black community made up just 8 percent of the population in Fort Myers compared to 15 percent throughout the rest of Florida. Buchanon, like his peers, fell into his comfort zone in Atlanta.

That changed in an instant while he was sitting in his condo during that fateful early morning on March 13, 2006. Buchanon heard a car pull into his driveway. He heard four car doors slam. A few seconds later, he saw his front door fly open.

In ran the five masked men. Or was it four? Adrenaline muddied the memories.

One of men pistol-whipped Buchanon. He hit Buchanon in the face with his gun. Another shoved a gun into Buchanon's mouth. They carried out two flat-screen TVs. Except for the ones he wore, they took his clothes. Then they stole Buchanon's car. Buchanon suspected he knew his assailants, who never were caught. Atlanta police eventually recovered the car, a green Porsche Cayenne sport-utility vehicle.

"My head was bleeding," Buchanon said. "I would never wish that on anybody else. They took everything of value in the house. I basically remained calm during the situation. The whole thing took about an hour and thirty minutes."

The entire incident could have been worse. He could have been injured. Or he could have been killed. Buchanon had built walls of distrust around him before this incident. After it, he retreated into a personal fortress of solitude.

"I don't put nothing past nobody anymore," said Buchanon, who has never been married or engaged. He had no children, and his level of trust for others played into that. "Guys, girls, it could be anybody. Anybody can set you up. Once you make it to the NFL, you're automatically a target."

Buchanon rid himself of the Atlanta home and rediscovered his true comfort zone in Miami. He still made side trips to Fort Myers. Unlike Earnest Graham and Jevon Kearse, who had established charity foundations and organized annual fund-raisers, Buchanon kept a lower profile while still giving back to his community. He paid summer camp entry fees for thirty high school football players, ten from Dunbar High, ten from Lehigh, and ten from East Lee County High, where his father had worked. He also bought new uniforms for three local Pop Warner football and cheerleading teams, never once calling the *News-Press* for publicity.

Buchanon cut back on his extravagant expenses as well. He once owned "a handful" of cars. Then he owned just two: the Cayenne in Miami and a black Range Rover he kept in the cities in which he played.

"If somebody sees somebody with a million dollars, they are rich to them," Buchanon said. "But guess what? Once you get the million dollars, and Uncle Sam comes in, you have $600,000. Once you get into buying a nice car and a nice house, you go from being a millionaire to having $100,000 or $200,000 at the most.

"If you just go out and are spending money and having fun—if you go out there and spend money like there's no tomorrow—you're going to be in trouble. Now if you can make it to my situation, I'm the perfect example. I made financial decisions I shouldn't have made back then. But at the same time, I had to do that in order to learn from that. A lot of people don't make it to their fourth year. Fortunately for me, I did. Here's what I learned: If you get bonus money, you shouldn't even touch that money. At least that money is safe, and at least you're making some kind of money off it.

"It's kind of hard, because guys get into the league. They play the first two or three years, and they're having fun. They don't think of the big picture. I was like that. At the same time, I was looking for advice."

The robbery at gunpoint changed Buchanon's outlook. He took to preparing for life after the NFL by attending the league's Business Management and Entrepreneurial Program. He began to put his millions to use. Consider: He signed a five-year, $12.5 million contract as a rookie with the Oakland Raiders that carried him through his tenure with the Houston Texans and Tampa Bay Buccaneers. He received a two-year, $8.5 million deal from the Detroit Lions, who released Buchanon before the second season of that contract could kick in. Entering 2010, Buchanon signed a one-year, $1.5 million deal with the Washington Redskins. He retired after spending 2011 with the Redskins as well.

Prior to retiring, Buchanon began to buy real estate. By 2009, he had purchased a number of commercial properties in Texas, Georgia, Florida, and Massachusetts. Businesses such as Joe's Crab Shack and Arby's restaurants leased properties owned by Buchanon. In addition to his NFL paychecks, Buchanon began to receive even more money as a landlord to restaurants and other businesses, including a day-care center. As of 2014, Buchanon also had created an Internet startup called tappish.com, and he had produced graphic novels.

"I want to turn $2 million into $4 million and then $4 million into $8 million and then $8 million into $16 million," Buchanon said. "I love to learn things. I've always been determined to figure things out. It's all about, 'How fast can I get my money back?'"

While putting together all of these business deals, Buchanon never forgot his primary purpose as a professional football player. He spent many an off-season in the University of Miami strength-and-conditioning room, working out with a large cast of former Hurricane players who also had made it to the pros. They migrated to that weight room each summer like birds returning home from the winter.

Buchanon accomplished plenty as an athlete.

As a senior in high school, he compiled 102 tackles, 2 sacks, and 7 interceptions and returned 3 punts for touchdowns. On offense, he rushed 115 times for 928 yards (8.0 yards per carry) and 13 touchdowns and caught 15 passes for 289 yards and 3 touchdowns.

As a senior in baseball, he hit .463 with 7 triples, 6 doubles, and 5 home runs. As a senior in basketball, he averaged 20.1 points, 5.5 assists, and 4.3 steals per game. In track, he ran the 100-meter dash in 10.5 seconds and the 200 meters in 21.8 seconds.

In three seasons at Miami, Buchanon intercepted 7 passes and returned 2 punts for touchdowns.

"I was just playing football there," Buchanon said of his three college seasons that did not include much actual focus on college. "Turning pro early gave me an extra year to be in the league and actually learn something. I thought I was going to be a top 10 pick. I ended up being No. 17. It doesn't get any better or worse than that."

In ten NFL seasons, Buchanon intercepted 20 passes, 5 of which he returned for touchdowns.

Critics of Buchanon accused him of being a soft tackler. But Buchanon compiled 348 tackles, averaging almost 35 per season over ten years. He showed no signs of decline until 2011, when he received a four-game suspension from the NFL for undisclosed rules violations. He finished his final season on injured reserve with a neck injury, appearing in just one game.

Buchanon's body of work as an NFL player provided more proof that his challenging upbringing could be overcome. Not far from Buchanon's house on Bert Drive lived another future NFL player bound for Lehigh Senior High School. This behemoth of a prospect would have an even more challenging path to the NFL than Buchanon.

Mario's Mission

Mario Henderson used to eat breakfast, lunch, and dinner at McDonald's. As he ate and ate the fast food, he grew and grew into supersized proportions. As a freshman at Bishop Verot High School, Henderson stood six foot four and weighed 300 pounds.

"Whenever we went on the road to play, we always made Mario get off the bus first, so that the opposing team would see him," said Mike Gill, Mario's freshman football coach. "The hardest thing about coaching Mario is that you forgot that he was just a fourteen-year-old kid. He had the body of a twenty-seven-year-old.

"I remember one time I yelled at him for doing something wrong. A minute or two later, I couldn't find him. He was trying to hide behind a telephone pole, crying. I said, 'Mario, what's the matter?' He said, 'You yelled at me, Coach. You were mean to me.'"

Not every NFL-bound player from Dunbar had to deal with the temptations to sell or use drugs or deal with the murder of a family member. Henderson grew up without a father and experienced the death of his mother at an early age. His burgeoning weight became one of his biggest problems.

By Henderson's junior year in high school, the future NFL offensive left tackle stood six foot seven and weighed 375 pounds. His skyrocketing weight would have gone even higher had he not played basketball.

"I used to eat twenty McDonald's cheeseburgers every day," said Henderson, who attended Bishop Verot High School as a freshman and sophomore. It took Henderson less than ten minutes to walk from the private Catholic school to the McDonald's at the corner of Summerlin Road and Colonial Boulevard. "I should own some of that property with as much money as I spent there."

Once a week cheeseburgers cost just twenty-nine cents, so Henderson usually bought them in bulk.

"I could find thirty cents on the ground and buy one," he said. "I had nothing else to do but sit there and eat. And they were good. And everybody knows that McDonald's makes the best breakfasts in the world. We all know that."

Born on October 29, 1984, Henderson grew up in suburban Chicago, never knowing his father. His mother, Sonia Henderson, was dating two men at the same time of her pregnancy. At age seventeen, she did not know which of the two men had fathered her son. She did not want to endure the indignity or the embarrassment of approaching either man for child support, especially since one of the men was married.

Instead, Sonia Henderson raised her son with the help of her parents, Herbert and Floridia Pickens.

"I've never met my father," said Henderson, who sometimes wonders who and where his father might be.

"You have to have a daddy out there somewhere," he said with a shrug. Sadly, Mario did not have a mom for long either. Between Mario's eighth and ninth birthday, Sonia Henderson learned she had breast cancer.

"We were young," Mario said. "She was seventeen when she had me, so she was like twenty-six. Since I was younger, I didn't really know what was going on. I remember the ambulance coming to the house. We were there with her. I remember everybody was like panicking. I remember we called my auntie. I remember my grandma saying something, that I might not see my mom again. But I was a young kid. I didn't know what was going on. I think she passed away later that night."

Henderson often astounded his mother and grandmother with his impromptu solo walks across Chicago.

"He has always been an adventurous person," Floridia Pickens said. "He was not afraid to go places. He one time walked fifteen blocks from his school to home. Another time, his mom was asleep. He always liked to come over and see me, because he knew I usually would take him somewhere to do something fun. He walked thirty blocks away, from his house to mine. In the snow."

After Sonia Henderson's death, the Pickens family relocated to Florida, where Floridia had grown up. She graduated from the all-black Dunbar High School in 1965. Floridia Pickens worked as a nurse, leaving Oak Park Hospital in Illinois for Lee Memorial Hospital in Fort Myers. Herbert Pickens left his job with the Chicago Transit Authority but was quite happy to return to Florida, where he could resume his hobby of fishing and continue bowling. They lived, in 1997, on Henderson Avenue, the same street on which Deion Sanders grew up but on the south side of Martin Luther King Jr. Boulevard.

"We had always planned on coming back here," Floridia Pickens said, sitting on the couch of her three-bedroom home in Lehigh Acres, where the family eventually moved and where she keeps her grandson's room intact. Henderson's feet hung well off the double bed he slept in during part of his off-seasons.

"We didn't want to deal with all of the bad weather," Floridia Pickens said of Chicago. "And we didn't want to move them when they were sixteen or seventeen. That's why we left when we did."

Moving back to Fort Myers with Henderson on the verge of his teenage years had a remarkable effect on the man-child.

"I met a lot of friends I'm still cool with to this day," Henderson said. "The area is not all good, but it's always what you make of it. There was a house like three doors down, and you could see stuff going on there. We were told to stay away from there.

"I was always playing either football or basketball, so that kept me away from that. I was playing on a traveling team, so I would stay at my friend's house in Cape Coral. I got a chance to see how I wanted to make a better life for myself."

The drug dealers influenced Henderson by providing an example of what he did not want to do.

"I don't question them for what they do," Henderson said. "I don't judge them for what they do."

Mario grew up with his uncle Brandon Pickens, who is a year and a half younger than Mario but did not play football. They were raised as brothers, and Mario did not usually call Floridia Pickens "Grandma." He called her "Mama."

When Sonia Henderson was still alive, Mario told her, "Mom, I'm going to call you Mommy." Then he turned to Floridia and said, "I'm going to call you Mama."

The Pickens family eventually settled in Lehigh Acres, a community of about seventy thousand just east of Fort Myers, where Mario Henderson spent his middle school years often getting into fights at school.

"The first year was really hard for him," Floridia Pickens said. "He had the adjustment of not being at home with nothing familiar around him."

Henderson attributed this to part of the grieving process.

"You know how kids in school would make mama jokes and talk about your mom?" he said. "Well, when they did that with me, that was one of the things that set me off. I was in third or fourth grade, and I used to get into fights all the time. My grandma never got mad at me, because she knew what I was going through. The last time it happened, I was in the eighth grade. A dude was talking about my mom."

Soon, Henderson transferred that aggression to sports. He just could not do it yet in football.

"I was too heavy," he said. Pop Warner football teams have maximum weight limits for each age group. "From day one, I was too big. Too big."

Fortunately for Mario, there were no weight limits in basketball.

"It didn't bother me, because all of my friends around me played basketball," Henderson said. "I played basketball more. I liked that sport better at the time anyway."

Mario muses that had his mother not died, the aggression in him might have remained dormant. Had he not been so heavy, he probably would have been pushed into football and away from basketball, which would have hindered his development as a football player.

"When we got Mario, we told him, 'Use basketball to help your football abilities,'" said his high school basketball coach at Lehigh, Mark Morehead. Mario transferred to Lehigh from Bishop Verot after his sophomore year. "Use it for your footwork. Use it for your agility. I'm talking about him playing for the Chicago Bears at that point, like it was a pipe dream. But we were just trying to get him to the next level."

Henderson helped lead Lehigh to consecutive district championships in basketball in 2001–2 and 2002–3, averaging 14 points and 11 rebounds as a senior.

"I thought he would end up in the NBA," Floridia Pickens said.

Sitting at the dining room table at a friend's Cape Coral home, just two days before departing for Napa Valley, California, site of the 2009 Oakland Raiders training camp, Henderson pondered a what-if.

"It's crazy," Henderson said. "Everything happens for a reason. If my mom hadn't died, I probably wouldn't have moved here. I probably wouldn't have fallen in love with sports."

Mario said he would trade everything to have his mother back. He has her name tattooed on his left forearm along with a cross rising above it and a pair of hands clasped together in prayer above that. They are three of the forty-some tattoos blanketing his upper body and neck.

"I always think about what my mom would be doing now," Henderson said. "I always wish she was here."

Before high school, Henderson attended Mount Hermon Christian School near downtown Fort Myers.

"They had flag football," he said. "They didn't have any weight classes for that."

So Mario got to play.

"A lot of my decisions had to do with sports," Henderson said. "That gave me some opportunities. And also, they had a basketball team."

Immersed into AAU basketball, a friend of Mario's encouraged him to attend Bishop Verot, which had a student body of about seven hundred.

That AAU team, the Wildcats, also included a tall, gangly power forward named Micah Rucker, who would grow into an NFL prospect himself. Rucker, who played at Estero High, spent parts of 2008 and 2009 on the Pittsburgh Steelers, Kansas City Chiefs, and New York Giants practice squads after playing college football at the University of Minnesota and Eastern Illinois.

Henderson received one of his earliest opportunities from Bishop Verot, which granted him full financial aid. He is still not exactly sure whom to thank.

"I remember twice a year, they would have me go down to the principal's office, and I would write a thank-you note," Henderson said. "My grandma, she worked from 7:00 a.m. to 7:00 p.m. as a nurse at Lee Memorial. I would have to go to Bishop Verot at like 6:30 in the morning. I would sit outside the gym until 9:00 a.m. Eventually, they would let me in. At night, because I had practices, I would still have to sit there another hour or an hour and a half, waiting for her to pick me up."

To kill time, Mario would walk to that McDonald's.

In the morning, he would order a sausage biscuit sandwich or two. Or three. He would return in the afternoon for a post-practice meal.

"I was worried about his health by him getting that big," his grandmother said. "I would tell him not to eat so much fatty food. He just ate a lot."

While many future NFL offensive linemen start with a 240-pound frame in high school and look to build their bulk before entering college, Mario weighed closer to 400 pounds as a senior. He needed to subtract.

Not until he arrived at Florida State University did Henderson learn to avoid McDonald's. By the end of his time as a Seminole, Henderson had dropped to 310 pounds. The weight loss positioned him as a midround NFL prospect. The Raiders took note, selecting Henderson in the third round of the 2007 draft, making him the ninety-first overall pick.

"He was about 360 pounds of fat and cheeseburgers," Larry Gary recalled of Henderson. "He was young. McDonald's took care of Bishop Verot. He was in an environment where they all went out there to eat. He had no discipline in watching what he ate. Eating habits are vital, especially in the NFL. At Florida State, I think it was just Mario figuring it out. He knew he had to get faster. I thought he had the potential of going to the pros. He was big enough. Mario was very agile for his size. Mario was thought of more highly because of his footwork and his reach."

Henderson said just making it to Florida State amazed him, especially after not handling the academics well at either Bishop Verot or Lehigh.

By the middle of his sophomore year at Bishop Verot, Henderson said, he struggled not just with the academics but with fitting in at the school.

"I was getting in trouble a lot," Henderson said. "I stole somebody's wallet. I did that all for one dollar. That was probably my most embarrassing moment. I went to school the next day, and everybody was just looking at me differently. I got suspended. I had to go through all of that.

"Everybody acted like I was some kind of a criminal. Well, I was, but it was a one-time thing. If you do it once, you have to learn from it."

Midway through his sophomore year, Henderson wanted a fresh start. He got one by transferring across town to Lehigh Senior High School, a public school of about 2,100 students in Lehigh Acres.

"He was really a pleasure to work with," said Mike Gill, Mario's freshman coach. "We really missed him when he left."

Jim Scarry, Bishop Verot's varsity coach during Mario Henderson's time at the school, has coached football for more than twenty-five years. Henderson remains the only player Scarry has coached to make an NFL roster.

"You knew he was special," said Scarry, whose father, Mo Scarry, coached in the NFL as an assistant for twenty-seven years, including a long stint under Hall of Fame Miami Dolphins coach Don Shula. "Did I think then that he would end up in the NFL? No. But did it surprise me when he did? No, it didn't surprise me. He was a big kid, but tremendously athletic. At that point in time, Mario really preferred basketball. We had him playing more defense than offense as a sophomore. He didn't have to do things correctly in order to be successful. He had those long arms, and he would just reach around guys to make tackles, but without the proper form.

"He would say, 'Why am I being yelled at? I made the tackle.' Those long arms are one of the reasons why he made it to the league. He has those great, long arms that are great for pass blocking.

"Another reason for Mario's success was his grandparents. They were so supportive of his education and of his coaches. They were just strong in that way. They were very respectful and humble."

At the end of Henderson's sophomore year at Bishop Verot, Larry Gary, then an assistant coach on Bishop Verot's staff, was offered a chance to return to Lehigh as the head coach. Gary took that opportunity, not realizing what it would mean to Henderson.

Two years earlier, Gary, the first coach at Lehigh, was not retained by the school as its football coach but stayed there as a teacher. Gary continued coaching but as an assistant at Bishop Verot. The same year Gary began coaching at Verot, a handful of Lehigh Senior High players transferred from Lehigh to Bishop Verot as well. Allegations of recruiting violations ensued.

"Bishop Verot and Lehigh had always bumped heads," Henderson said. "The fact that it happened with them and then it appeared to be happening with me, it raised red flags."

The flags were so red in Henderson's case that the Florida High School Athletic Association would not allow Henderson to play his junior season at Lehigh because of a rule prohibiting players from being eligible for one year if they follow a head coach to another school.

To this day, Henderson insists Gary did not lure him to Lehigh.

"I had already done the school-choice thing," Henderson said. "When Coach Gary made the move to Lehigh, I was already there."

Henderson got to practice as a junior but could not play varsity football.

"When they had the scout offense out, I played defense, and I played hard," Henderson recalled. "Practices were like games to me."

When Gary held practices without pads, Henderson wore pads anyway.

"Why are you practicing with pads on in the 100-degree heat?" Henderson would be asked. "I was out there every freaking day, working for free."

Having shed some of his McDonald's weight, Henderson joined coach Mark Morehead's basketball team at Lehigh weighing close to 330 pounds, down from 375.

Morehead, a Chicago native and die-hard Cubs fan, grew up one town over from Henderson's mother. Sonia Henderson grew up in Bellwood, Illinois, and Morehead lived in Westchester. In a strange coincidence, Morehead and Sonia Henderson each attended Proviso West High, although at different times. When Morehead learned he would be adding a six-foot-seven junior—from suburban Chicago, no less—to his basketball roster, he felt as if he had won the lottery.

"He was in the good 320s when we got him," Morehead said. "We had to go get extra uniforms, because I didn't have anything that would fit him. We just tried to help him become better. We don't beat Fort Myers High very often. We were playing a preseason game against them his junior year. We had the game going the way we wanted to. All of a sudden, he makes this idiotic foul. I'm like, 'Mario, what are you doing?' He said he was tired and had to stop the game, and that's why he fouled.

"I'll never forget that. I couldn't get mad at him. I just said, 'Tell me next time, and we'll call a timeout, and we'll get you out.'

"We helped get him in shape so he could play spring football. Mario did all the work. Mario did the running. We don't win the first district championship without Mario Henderson in there. We don't win the second one without Mario Henderson in there. He did a lot more for us than we ever did for him. We're all grateful for having the opportunity to have that kid around us."

All of that work on the basketball court helped make up for Henderson's lack of varsity football experience.

With just one season of varsity action—his senior year—Henderson was being hounded by two of the country's top Division I football coaches at the same time, Tommy Bowden at Clemson and his father, Bobby Bowden, at Florida State.

"I used to tell Mario when I was there, 'You do everything right, and Bobby Bowden is going to visit us one day,'" said Jim Scarry, a Florida State graduate. "Of course, we both weren't at Verot when that happened, but it happened."

The recruiting hype that surrounded Henderson surprised him.

"It was weird, because I didn't have any film," Henderson said. "Football season was over with. They didn't offer me a scholarship until three weeks into the year. It was January 18."

Henderson almost didn't qualify for a scholarship. His grades had not improved, even after transferring from Bishop Verot. He scored just a 740 on his SAT. He recalled his grade-point average as between 1.5 and 1.7. He needed to boost that closer to 3.0.

Midway through his senior year, after football season had ended, Henderson transferred from Lehigh to Academy High, where students can make up poor grades and earn a diploma through General Education Development (GED).

The Clemson coaching staff, thinking it had the chance to land Henderson, helped orchestrate Henderson's transfer to the Academy so he could get eligible.

Henderson assured Clemson coach Tommy Bowden he would sign with the Tigers. But then Florida State's Bobby Bowden suddenly made a personal visit to Lehigh Senior High. On January 29, 2003, Bowden sat in a Lehigh office, waiting for Henderson to arrive from the Academy.

"Bobby came in that morning, and Mario committed," Mark Morehead said. "That same afternoon, Tommy came in. FSU wanted to play him right away. Clemson wanted to redshirt him. The dog-and-pony show went on with Bobby. Then we had to deal with the ramifications of Tommy Bowden showing up later in the afternoon. It was a bizarre day."

Henderson credited Morehead with keeping him in shape through the vigorous basketball workouts. Henderson credited Larry Gary with helping him get eligible for college. "I didn't even realize it at the time," Henderson said, "but he worked so hard for me."

Off Henderson went to Florida State. He went there unprepared, physically and academically.

When I asked Henderson about his college major, he laughed.

"I majored in eligibility," he said.

Eligibility?

"That was pretty much my degree," said Henderson, who did not graduate from college. Meeting the minimum academic requirements to remain eligible for football turned into Henderson's goals. He failed to reach that goal as a freshman.

"At the end of my freshman year, my GPA was 0.9," Henderson said. "Back then, they had a thing called forgiveness. They wipe it off. The bad thing is, those credits are useless. You could only do it once."

Henderson did not play much as a freshman or a sophomore, although he did get his first varsity start during the Orange Bowl against Miami.

As a sophomore, Henderson learned he needed at least a 1.9 GPA in order to maintain his scholarship. He ended the year with a 2.9 GPA.

"That was pretty good," Henderson said. "My sophomore year, I started picking up the books. I had a million talks about losing my scholarship. They were paying for everything. I got mad at myself, because when that happened, I lost all of my free time. I had to do hours and hours of study hall. I had to do my projects early a lot of the time, just to get everything done. I brought it upon myself. You mature a lot more between the ages of eighteen and twenty. That's how it was for me."

Henderson began to mature more in football as well.

"I started the last two games of my junior year," he said. "I thank God every day. I just wanted to hang in there and see what would happen. I still loved football. I thought, even if I don't play another down at Florida State, I was still going to make an effort to try."

Floridia Pickens remains so proud of her grandson.

"As he got into football, he began to like it more," she said. "He started to work hard at it. He worked very, very hard. He's a very focused person."

All of Henderson's effort paid off in his senior season, when he vaulted onto the NFL left-tackle prospects list. Left tackles fill the crucial role of protecting a right-handed quarterback's blind side. "Opportunities in the NFL don't last that long," Henderson said. "Sometimes you forget what the NFL stands for—Not For Long."

Henderson, listed at 308 pounds following his third NFL season, set a goal to earn a more lucrative contract upon becoming a free agent entering the 2011 season. He made $460,000 in 2009 and $550,000 in 2010.

"I bought a lot of things because I could afford them," Henderson said. "I bought shoes. I bought a lot of shoes, and I don't even wear them. Last I looked, I had thirty-seven pairs of Jordans. I mostly buy Air Jordans. I bought the retros. Like a pair from his rookie year in 1984. I've got like seven pairs of them. I don't do that as much as I used to."

Henderson also bought three vehicles: a black Cadillac Escalade he leaves in Florida, a black Chrysler 300 he had in California while with the Oakland Raiders, and a nice, old-school car for his free time—a 1973 burnt-orange Impala.

"I like the look of that," he said. "I like the frame."

Entering 2011, however, Henderson had issues with his own frame. He fell off the weight wagon. He headed back toward 400 pounds again. The Raiders took one look at Henderson following the NFL lockout of 2011 and sent him back to Lehigh Acres without a contract. Henderson spent 2011 trying to lose weight. He went from cashing weekly $40,000 NFL paychecks to making two hundred dollars a week during a three-week stint with the Colorado Ice of the Indoor Football League. In 2012, Henderson dropped Drew Rosenhaus as his agent and became the only client of Kansas City, Missouri–based Tim Rogers, who found Henderson a training camp invitation with the San Diego Chargers.

The Chargers cut Henderson just prior to the 2012 season. He played the 2014 season with the Tampa Bay Storm of the Arena Football League. As Henderson's NFL journey came to a close, he still had valuable memories from his past.

On January 13, 2009, Lehigh invited Henderson back home to retire his basketball jersey. Coach Morehead presented Henderson with a framed number 32 Lightning basketball jersey at the ceremony. Another such jersey hangs in the school's gymnasium.

"When these kids move on and become successful, and they come back, you've got to reward them," Morehead said. "What he has done opens doors for so many other kids here."

Henderson credited Fort Myers with giving him the foundation and the fuel to propel himself to the NFL. He would not be the only big man from Dunbar destined to make it.

Terrence Triumphs

Terrence Cody grabbed a teammate and took him to the ground. That meant a mass standing six foot four and weighing 405 pounds was smothering a five-foot, nine-inch, 240-pound teammate. Cody did this on the first day of spring football practice his junior year at Riverdale High School, May 2004.

"Terrence had him totally covered," said Scott Jones, Riverdale's coach at the time. "I said, 'You can't do that anymore. I don't want you laying out a kid on our team.'" So Jones instituted a separate set of rules for Cody. The Cody Rules forbade him from tackling during practice. Cody instead would wrap up opposing offensive players so he at least could work on tackling fundamentals.

The next play Cody made, he picked up the team's 240-pound fullback, threw him over his shoulder, and walked him over to Jones.

Cody did things Jones had never seen a high school player do since he got into coaching in 1983, moving to Fort Myers from his native West Virginia. Upon taking the job at Riverdale, a high school about a twenty-minute drive east of Dunbar, Jones saw little of Cody on the football field because he had been ruled academically ineligible as a sophomore and in the fall of his junior year. Cody spent his time after school at home, playing video games and watching his little brother while their mother worked as a school bus driver.

"I had him in PE classes and playing basketball," Jones said of Cody. Despite the excess weight, Cody could slam-dunk. Jones told Cody's mother, "If he does the right thing, he could be making millions of dollars in about eight years."

Cody proved Jones correct. After the Baltimore Ravens selected Cody in the second round of the 2010 NFL Draft with the fifty-seventh overall pick, Cody signed a four-year, $3.385 million contract, which included a guaranteed $1.2 million signing bonus.

Years before helping the Ravens win the Super Bowl on February 3, 2013, in the Mercedes-Benz Superdome, Cody yearned to play high school football. Before his junior year, he approached Jones and asked him what he had to do in order to play.

"That January, he got eligible," Jones said. "He played spring ball his junior year. He was 405. I told him he needed to get down to 365 within about three months. Dude, he can eat, man. Some kids drink. Some kids do drugs. Well, he ate. I saw him eat fifty wings one time. All the teachers liked him. He was never in trouble. He was personable. When he finally got to his senior year, he was a tremendous impact player. He was six feet, four inches and 380 pounds. Nobody's going to block him. So we put him on the goal line."

Long before June 28, 1988, when Cody entered the world, forces began to shape his upbringing. Cody's existence in Dunbar indirectly began on a Georgia cotton field. His paternal grandmother, Elizabeth Cody, began toiling in the field at age six. Born on January 23, 1943, Liz Cody picked cotton near her childhood home of Colquitt, Georgia, alongside her brothers Tommy and Willie.

"We picked a lot of cotton," Liz Cody said, as she watered her garden at her Fort Myers home. "And my brother Tommy? My brother could pick cotton. He could pick cotton so fast."

Liz Cody moved to Fort Myers in her youth and witnessed the lure of drugs all around her. The drugs briefly entrapped her oldest son, Terrence Cody's father. She also suffered the emotional scars others in Dunbar had faced. Her father abandoned her when she was a child. She relocated with her mother, Effie, to Fort Myers and to a Market Street home in Dunbar after Cecil Cody left the family. Liz Cody attended Dunbar High School in the early 1960s before finishing her high school education in Georgia, back with her father after reuniting with him.

"I very much disliked my daddy because of what he did to us," Liz Cody said of her father leaving. "But his mother—my grandmother—I loved her dearly. He called down here and got in touch with me, and I went up there to finish high school."

Liz Cody graduated from the all-black Blakely High in 1963. She then returned to Fort Myers, where she embarked on a life of hard work, cooking, and bearing eight children with two men. She kept her maiden name of Cody, and she had her first child, Terrence Cody Sr., on March 3, 1964, less than a year after graduating from high school. All of her children's names and birthdates she etched into the concrete patio of her home, from where she could view the grapevine, collard greens, and royal palms she planted after moving there in the late 1980s.

Liz Cody's eight children enabled her to become a grandmother to twenty-two and a great-grandmother to six by the age of sixty-eight. Before retiring to tend to her garden, Liz Cody worked three jobs at one time. She worked with mentally challenged youth at the Gulf Coast Center for thirty-five years. Terrence Cody Sr. attended North Fort Myers High School, overlapping part of his time there with Deion Sanders. Cody Sr., who graduated from North in 1983, never played football, and he had his mother to blame for that.

"He wanted to play football in his younger years," Liz Cody said. "I was scared for him to play, so I wouldn't let him."

Before becoming a father to Terrence Cody Jr., Cody Sr. ended up taking the wrong path on the streets of Dunbar.

"He dibbled and dabbled, selling drugs," Liz Cody said. He got involved with a dealer nicknamed Rosco. Cody Sr. then ended up getting arrested. The charges never stuck, and Liz Cody believed the experience scared him straight. "We kept talking to him," Liz Cody said. "I never liked that kind of stuff. I believe that woke him up."

Cody the pro football player learned of his father's misdeeds later in life. They served as a valuable lesson to him.

"I knew about that," Cody said. "My mom told me. But at the end of the day, he gave that up. I didn't live in a good neighborhood. With the surroundings I grew up in, you were able to be in the wrong place at the wrong time."

After Terrence Cody Sr. ended his dabbling with drugs, he found honest work. He did so in the fast-food restaurant business, working his way up to manager status. If a fried-chicken franchise existed in Fort Myers, the odds were pretty good that Cody Sr. had managed it. Popeyes, Church's, KFC—Cody managed them all. He also managed Checkers and a Hardee's.

"I'm so glad," Liz Cody said. "I'm so glad he turned to honest work. You don't have to worry about going to jail from those kinds of jobs."

Cody Sr. did not stay married to Linnea Alexander, the mother of Cody Jr., but he maintained a presence in his son's life. He once set up an account at a Pizza Hut, allowing Cody Jr. and his sisters to eat as they pleased. When Cody Jr. lost his father, it happened not because of neglect but because of an accident.

On October 13, 2000, Cody Sr. was driving on State Road 31 near Arcadia, about forty-five miles to the northeast of Fort Myers. His girlfriend, her two daughters, and a niece were in the car when a truck collided with it head-on. Cody Sr. died instantly. The others were injured and later recovered. Cody Jr., who was twelve at the time, had a tough time recovering from the emotional trauma. His mother cried when talking about having to tell her four children their father had died.

"I woke them up at two o'clock in the morning," Linnea Alexander said. "I couldn't sleep. I got them all into the living room." Her daughters were crying. Her youngest son, Tabias, three years old at the time, was confused and did not realize the impact of what had happened.

As for twelve-year-old Terrence, "he just sat there," Alexander said. "When he first found out, he didn't cry or nothing. I said, 'T—are you understanding what I'm saying?' He said, 'Yes, ma'am.' Even at the wake, he didn't cry at the wake. But at the funeral, he finally broke down and started crying."

"He had a real big place in my life," Cody said. "Sometimes, my mom and I would argue when I was growing up. He was always the person I would call when I got mad about things. I'd call him and talk to him. He was a real big influence on my attitude. When he passed away, it was hard on me. In high school, I started getting myself together. I wish he could have been there when I started playing football. I wish he could have seen where I am now."

Alexander and her oldest son played a part in raising each other. Alexander's mom, Terry Florence, was fourteen when Alexander was born. Alexander was seventeen when she gave birth to Terrence. They grew up in some of the poorest neighborhoods of Dunbar. Alexander often had two to three low-paying jobs. She worked as a hostess at the Bob Evans restaurant on Daniels Parkway, as a certified nurse's assistant, and as a bus driver for the Lee County School District.

Mother and son did not always get along.

"He tried to run away," Liz Cody said.

One time Cody showed up at his grandmother's house and started to play video games as if nothing had happened. A police officer soon arrived looking for Cody, because his mother had reported he ran away from home.

"The door's always open to all my children and grandchildren," Liz Cody said with a smile.

Cody's desire to leave that Washington Avenue home—it was not far from where fellow big man Mario Henderson lived and where Phillip Buchanon grew up on Bert Drive—stemmed from the crime and chaos surrounding him there. Cody learned to avoid a nearby neighbor's house because of the drugs sold there.

"It's my home, and it's my birthplace," Cody said of Fort Myers. "There's a lot of struggling on the streets. Sometimes it seems like there's nothing to do but get into trouble. I think that's what pushes everybody to try and get out of there."

In May 2004, Cody began spending more time with a junior teammate. Jason Milliken, who is white and played offensive guard for the Riverdale Raiders, arrived in his red pickup truck to Washington Avenue almost every day in order to take Cody to or from football practice. On one of those days, a drug dealer mistook Milliken for someone looking to buy marijuana.

As the dope dealer approached Milliken, Linnea Alexander emerged from her home wielding a broom. She swung the broom at the dealer, warding him off and away from Milliken.

"They learned not to give him any problems," Alexander said. "They learned to respect him."

Soon, Cody learned to respect the Milliken family, which ended up taking him into their North Fort Myers home, not far from where Jevon Kearse had once lived with the family of Cisco Navas, years earlier.

"There wasn't much room for me, because it was just a two-bedroom apartment," Cody said of the living conditions with his mother. What began as several sleepovers evolved into a new home and a second family.

"I ended up just living with them after a couple of months," Cody said. "They ended up taking me in. My mom couldn't do for me what I needed. That really helped me my senior year. They didn't want my mom thinking that they wanted to take me away from her. They adopted me because my mom couldn't do all of the things they could do. Me and my mom, we're still good."

Maureen and Robert Milliken owned a stucco business and Disaster Restoration Squad, which overhauled homes damaged by fire, floods, mold, or other calamities. They also owned land in rural Alva, where Jason Milliken and Cody rode four-wheel drive all-terrain vehicles, chasing one another for fun.

The Millikens provided more than just a structure for Cody. They provided regular meals, a positive environment, and a place where he could thrive. They also provided him a queen-sized futon after his 400-pound frame broke the springs on their couch and recliner.

Jason Milliken relocated his bedroom to the room downstairs with Cody. They nicknamed it "the Cave," as they would crank the wall-unit air conditioner on full blast and play video games at a frenetic pace.

"Jason's his best friend," said Kourtney Kelley, Cody's girlfriend and mother of their daughter, Talia. "They have a bond. It is a very strong bond. They have had a positive impact on him. They have Terrence's best interests in mind. They love him. They see him as if he were their own flesh and blood. They've been nothing but nice. On Christmas, birthdays, holidays, they send cards and gifts. Some of our flesh-and-blood relatives don't even do that."

Cody made an impact on the Millikens as well. He secured Super Bowl tickets for all but daughter Mallory, who had just given birth to a baby girl. Cody sometimes called Maureen Milliken "Mom" and other times "Maureen."

"For as big of a guy he is, you'd never know he was around," she said. The warrior on the football field had a kind and gentle personality at home.

"It's almost like two different people, honest to God," Maureen Milliken said. "I think that's why many people underestimated him. But on the field, he can be a monster. I'd tell him, 'I don't want to meet you in a dark alley somewhere.' He'd say, 'Oh, come on, Maureen!'"

When Maureen Milliken described how she confirmed Cody as an official member of their household, she had tears in her eyes. The tale resembles the one told by author Michael Lewis in his best seller *The Blind Side*, but for Maureen Milliken, this was no book or Sandra Bullock movie. It's her life.

"You're here," she told Cody. "You're my child now. You're my son."

"Yes, ma'am," Cody said.

"Don't you 'yes, ma'am' me," she countered.

"Yes, ma'am," Cody replied. "I mean it."

Scott Jones, Cody's first football coach, said he was proud of Cody for staying away from drugs, focusing on his education and climbing through the challenges of junior college to the University of Alabama and then to the NFL. Cody won championships at all three of those stops.

"I think a lot of kids who come from that type of background, they want to make themselves better," Jones said. "He certainly did."

Two memories of coaching Cody at Riverdale stood out, Jones said. The first was buying four pairs of specialized pants for Cody, who could not fit into any other size.

The second was a tackle Cody made during a game in his senior season against North Fort Myers High. Playing in a storm that caused a two-hour rain-and-lightning delay, Cody lined up with the intent to tackle the most prolific high school running back in Lee County history.

This running back experienced the perils of Dunbar from all angles. He would go on to set Lee County rushing records. But on this night, he had to get past Cody. He could not. Noel Devine ran smack into Cody during an off-tackle play.

"Noel Devine was throwing up on the sidelines," Jones said of how hard Cody hit him. "I remember that play," Jason Milliken said. "Devine, for some reason, thought he could duck under Terrence. When Terrence landed on top of him, Devine started to bounce off him. But Terrence flattened him."

Cody recalled the hit with reverence for the player he tackled.

"He cut back, and I caught him," Cody said. "He was out for two quarters. All the seniors were happy because they didn't have to worry about him anymore."

Plenty of others would worry about Devine. He created problems in more ways than one.

Noel Devine

With a perfect name and a perfect game, Noel Devine is the perfect example of how growing up in Dunbar can shape one's destiny.

The name Noel evokes Christmas, a day of great joy, a day celebrating the birth of Christ. Devine serves as a homophone for divine, meaning godlike.

Put Noel and Devine together, and you've got quite a name and quite a football player. Nicknamed "Fro" by his friends and family, Devine demonstrated his football prowess even before becoming a teenager, capturing the imaginations of his Pop Warner coaches. Devine then launched himself from a youth football phenom to a high school star with one amazing play. The play helped shaped Devine's destiny, for without his amazing abilities, the attempted adoption by Deion Sanders, and the extra care he received from his teachers, coaches, and friends' parents might not have saved him from the harsher fates suffered by some of his friends.

The play happened his freshman season. From afar, he looked like he still could have been playing Pop Warner football, which many of his freshmen friends still did. Up close, Devine's muscles threatened to rip through his jersey. At age fifteen, he could bench-press 330 pounds. He could accelerate, stop in an instant, change directions and regain optimal speed in a flash. Devine did just that, multiple times, during a touchdown run after a catch that began his ascent to fame.

It unfolded like this: First down and 80 yards to go from the 20-yard line, sophomore quarterback Alvin Kelty dropped back to pass. Receivers sprinted up the field, while Devine hung back to block. After missing his block on purpose, Devine turned and caught the ball, right there on the 20-yard line. Three defenders already were behind Devine. That left eight more to beat and 80 yards to go.

Devine turned and broke to his left toward the sideline. He found himself in a one-on-one matchup against a linebacker. The linebacker made the first move, lunging and then diving for Devine's right ankle. Devine sidestepped to his left and sprinted forward again, leaving four men behind him, seven more to beat, and 75 yards to go.

Three steps and five yards later, Devine found himself in another one-on-one battle against a linebacker. Devine quickly cut back inside. The linebacker could not adjust his speed. The one-on-one battle turned into a two-on-one exchange. Devine won, with a teammate blocking the linebacker backward. That left five men down, six more to beat, and 70 yards to go.

The next defender forced Devine to slow down and run back to the outside in order to avoid the tackle. Devine's deceleration allowed the previous linebacker to get back into the picture. As that linebacker reached from behind to try to grab Devine's left arm, another defender ran forward and toward Devine like a runaway train. All of a sudden, Devine's feet lifted off the ground as if he wore a jet pack. Devine spun in the air like an Olympic figure skater would do in attempting a single, counterclockwise axel. One second later, the two defenders languished behind Devine. That left six men down, five more to beat, and 60 yards to go.

Up next: two more defenders. One lunged and dived for Devine's left ankle. He missed. That left seven men behind Devine. Two of them continued their relentless pursuit. Those two running from behind and two more forward-running defenders converged upon Devine at once. Again, they attempted to stop him. Again, they failed. Devine performed another spin move. This time, Devine used the momentum of the would-be tackler who rammed into him hard. Instead of trying to fight the force of the collision, Devine flowed with it, doing another counterclockwise spinning maneuver. That left eight men down, three more to beat, and 55 yards to go.

The ninth defender closed in on Devine. He sidestepped the safety, who reached for Devine's left ankle in vain. Nine men down, two more to beat, and 50 yards to go.

Right there, at the 50-yard line, Devine ran into another problem: his teammates. Six fellow red jerseys had converged near Devine's number 7 in an attempt to block for him. They almost knocked him down by accident. Devine eluded the traffic jam. He turned from north and south to east and west. He took two sidesteps, as if trying to squeeze through a narrow corridor. Once he got through, he turned north again. By then, his teammates had eliminated the remaining two defenders. That left eleven men behind him, no one to beat, and 45 yards to go.

Devine covered that with ease, sprinting to the end zone. He handed the ball to the nearest official and jogged back to the sideline. The play took twenty seconds, according to the game film, but all of that unfolded in what seemed like a split second while watching it live from the sidelines. In my twenty-plus-year career of covering high school football games, this remains the most exciting play I ever have seen firsthand. Devine and his teammates would go on to lose that game 34–20. When they walked off the field, they were buzzing with excitement over the 80-yard screen pass for a touchdown.

"You know what I told him?" James Iandoli, Devine's coach, asked me during the game's aftermath. "I said, 'That run was so good, it was stupid.' That's what the kids say. The kid's all heart. He's 175 pounds of heart. That's all he is. He doesn't stop. The kid doesn't stop."

"That's the best run I've ever seen," said Gary Kamphouse, an assistant coach. "I just said that twelve times."

The play would have made Devine an instant Internet legend, except that it unfolded on September 19, 2003. Youtube.com did not launch until February 2005. In the spring of 2004, Derek Williams of sunshinepreps.net had gotten hold of the clip. He posted it on his website. In one day, twenty thousand people clicked on the video, and Williams's server crashed. "The kid's unreal," Williams said. He called Devine's coach, wondering why Devine wasn't included on a list of rising seniors. "When he told me he was only going to be a sophomore, I about fell out of my chair," Williams said. "The kid's a freak of nature. There are no ifs, ands, or buts about it."

At five foot eight and 175 pounds, Devine stood an inch under the average height of an American male. "You don't see many fourteen- or fifteen-year-old kids who can bench-press 330 pounds," Williams said. "Maybe a 280-pound lineman. But you just don't see a 180-pound running back doing it."

Devine began his teenage years living with his maternal grandmother in Cape Coral, which led him to a youth football program there and later to North Fort Myers High. He spent his childhood years living on Dupree Street in Dunbar, literally a stone's throw from the new Dunbar High School and just south of Edison Avenue.

Born on February 16, 1988, Devine never knew his biological father, one of a pair of twins named Noel and Moel Devine. They also were running backs at North Fort Myers High, playing there because they lived in a Dunbar neighborhood designated as a feeder school for the Red Knights program. Drug users and drug dealers, Noel and Moel Devine each died from complications of the AIDS virus before Noel Devine could know them. Noel Devine told the *News-Press* he learned later in his life that Moel, not Noel, was his biological father.

Noel Devine began life under the care of his mother Abbigail, who would marry Mark Carter Sr. She died from complications of the AIDS virus when her son turned eleven. Part of a blended family, Devine often received advice and influence from his stepfather, who worked at the Star Service gas station in the 1970s in Dunbar, briefly crossing paths with Ronnie Tape. Mark Carter's father, Johnny Carter, also provided inspiration, standing out as a football player himself.

Johnny Carter, who was born on March 25, 1938, in Fort Myers, was raised in Dunbar after his father had moved there decades earlier, helping build the railroads that swooped in from the north, making the remote, western edge of the Everglades accessible.

Johnny Carter graduated from Dunbar High School in 1958. He went to Allen University, just as Green, Morrison, and Stephens had a decade earlier. The experience did not turn out for Carter as it did for his predecessors. "I tried out up there, I got hurt, and I had to come back home," Carter said. "I didn't have no scholarship. I didn't have the money to send me to college."

A torn knee ligament and no income did not stop Johnny Carter's determination to have a job and support his family. He commuted forty miles south to Naples for thirty-five years, working for the City of Naples as a garbage truck driver.

"I ran for a lot of touchdowns," Johnny Carter said of his Dunbar High days. "They called me Johnny 'Powerhouse' Carter. That was the nickname that I had. We played right there in Velasco Village. Nobody could ever tackle me, so that's the name they gave me."

Al Hixon, manager of the D and D Grocery Store, once challenged Johnny Carter, offering him a bag of twelve apples if he could score five touchdowns in one game on the road in Arcadia. Carter did just that.

Years later Noel Devine, whom Carter considers his grandson, even though they are not related by blood, surpassed "Powerhouse" Carter. As a sophomore, Devine rushed for 6 touchdowns on only 9 carries in one game. He finished that game with 365 yards, an average of 40.5 yards per carry, as North Fort Myers defeated Estero 63–7.

Devine had five half siblings in the children of his stepfather, Mark Carter Sr., a mechanic until a 1986 motorcycle accident injured his back. They all piled into that two-bedroom home on Dupree Street in Dunbar.

During those years, Devine was the baby of the blended family. At age six, he liked to sucker-punch brother Mark Carter Jr., before spending the rest of the day running away from him. Devine ran door to door in the neighborhood, asking his friends' parents for chocolate. Before their mother's death, Devine and his brothers played football in the Dupree Street cul-de-sac.

Mark Carter Sr. had been with Devine's mother before and after her affair with Devine's biological father.

"Oh, you know, lovers' quarrels," Carter Sr. said when asked why he was separated from Abbigail. The separation, as he recalled, lasted just a few weeks. A family portrait with the two of them surrounded by their children still hung in Carter Sr.'s living room more than a decade after her death. It hung next to yellowed, fading photographs of Noel Devine playing youth football.

After Abbigail died, her mother, Lee Thomas, took custody of Devine. Thomas moved her grandson out of the Carter house, which, Carter Sr. admitted, was too small for that many children. Lee Thomas had run-ins with the law as a convicted drug dealer, but by the late 1990s, she had pulled herself out of that life.

Devine often strayed from his grandmother's home. As a freshman and sophomore at North Fort Myers High, Devine began staying at the home of a white teammate named Robbie Harlowe. They were friends with former Cape Coral High School football player Alphonso Stewart, who would go on to spend time in prison on drug charges and would be murdered in the summer of 2011 in Fort Myers.

Stewart could have been killed years earlier. The same held true for Devine.

On December 30, 2004, shortly before 3:09 p.m. on Winsome Road in North Fort Myers, Devine and about fourteen friends, all around the age of fifteen, were looking to pick a fight with a fellow fifteen-year-old named Clyde Robinson Jr. The friends included Rashard Patterson, also fifteen. He became friends with Devine while playing for the same Pop Warner football team.

Robinson saw the throng of potential assailants outside. They wanted to beat him following a disagreement the day before over a girl-friend. He would have none of that. Robinson opened the front door. He walked onto the lawn. He carried with him a sawed-off shotgun with a pistol grip. Robinson fired it, and the shot flew straight into Patterson's gut. Patterson collapsed and died less than an hour later, slipping away on an emergency room operating table. Robinson went on to be convicted of second-degree manslaughter and sentenced to 10 years in prison.

Devine, standing only a few feet from the fired shot, fled with his friends.

The day changed the trajectory of Devine's life. It prompted North Fort Myers High School principal Steven DeShazo to take action. De-Shazo, who once paddled the backside of Deion Sanders for throwing an empty milk carton onto the roof of the school, reached out to Sanders, who was thirty-eight and in the middle of the second of two comeback seasons with the Baltimore Ravens. DeShazo implored Sanders to guide Devine. Devine and Sanders exchanged daily text messages and often spoke on the phone. Sanders made his intentions clear: to adopt the football prodigy and bring him to his family's Prosper home.

Deion Sanders set a plan in motion: to pick up Devine in late July, bring him to training camp with the Ravens, and then send Devine to Prosper, where he would play for the Prosper High School football team. It did not end well.

On July 28, 2005, in between Devine's sophomore and junior seasons, an adult friend of Devine's called 911, claiming Sanders was trying to kidnap Devine. No charges were filed, and Devine moved to Prosper with Sanders. The call foreshadowed what happened two weeks later, when Devine left Sanders's mansion. Devine took Pilar Sanders's SUV and left the car at Dallas/Fort Worth International Airport with the keys still in the ignition. Devine then flew back to Fort Myers and returned to the Harlowes' modest Cape Coral home.

Years later, Devine told the *News-Press* he regretted the way he left Sanders, but he did not regret leaving.

"I felt loved," Devine said. "I felt an unconditional love. I have a lot of respect for him. But when I got there, I missed home. I missed everything."

Devine said Sanders provided more than everything he needed, but it still wasn't enough.

"I had everything, but I still wasn't happy," Devine said. "It was a great experience. It was great motivation for me. I never would have made it this far if it weren't for him. He's a great role model."

Devine could not handle the distance from his Dunbar roots. He finished his high school football career and education where he began it. He finished it as Lee County's all-time leading rusher with 6,842 yards and 92 touchdowns, topping the yardage mark held before him by Earnest Graham.

In the spring of 2007, Devine graduated from North Fort Myers and secured a college football scholarship at West Virginia University. With the exception of keeping in contact with his closest relatives, his friends and his two—eventually, three—children, Devine had left his hometown behind him. He returned every so often, but he would do so in discreet and secretive fashion, as if trying to keep his hometown and the tales of his challenging childhood hidden.

Devine experienced his share of troubles, but he was safe and sound in Morgantown, West Virginia, on a late November night in 2007. This murderous night in Florida further demonstrated the dangers that could come from Dunbar.

The Tragic Death of Sean Taylor

Sean Taylor wasn't supposed to be at home. At 1:45 a.m. on Monday, November 26, 2007, the Washington Redskins safety, a former University of Miami Hurricane and a Miami native, should have been with his NFL teammates. They were back home near Washington, D.C., a few hours after returning from a 19–13 loss to the Tampa Bay Buccaneers on Sunday afternoon in Tampa. Earnest Graham rushed for a game-high 75 yards and a touchdown in that game. Phillip Buchanon forced a fumble and compiled 8 tackles, 7 solo, second-most on the team after linebacker Derrick Brooks's 9.

There were other Fort Myers natives preparing for action that day, far away from any football field.

Four Fort Myers residents and another from nearby Lehigh Acres were traveling not to Tampa but to Palmetto Bay, just south of Miami. That's where Taylor, nursing a knee injury that had forced him out of his team's two most recent games, stayed at home recuperating. The twenty-four-year-old All-Pro safety was spending time with his live-in girlfriend Jackie Garcia—a niece of the actor Andy Garcia—and their eighteen-month-old daughter.

In the earliest hours of that Monday, four teenagers and one twenty-year-old arrived from Fort Myers at Taylor's home, according to police reports. There, these young men, two of whom had played high school football, broke into the house, which had been burglarized one week before. They intended to burglarize it again, not realizing Taylor was at home.

According to the reports, one of the five young men stayed out of the house, waiting inside the car. The others found the master bedroom, startling Taylor, who grabbed a machete from under his bed in order to defend himself. As Taylor bolted into action, so did one of the young men, shooting Taylor in the leg. The bullet pierced the femoral artery. In his prime as a football player, Taylor died one day later, the loss of blood too great to overcome.

On Friday of that week, Miami detectives arrested twenty-year-old Venjah K. Hunte, eighteen-year-old Charles Wardlow, and seventeen-year-old Eric Rivera Jr., all of Fort Myers; and nineteen-year-old Jason Scott Mitchell of Lehigh Acres.

Wardlow and Rivera were raised in Dunbar neighborhoods, the sons of convicted drug dealers. Rivera grew up visiting his father of the same name in several federal prisons. Rivera Sr. spent the first ten years of his son's life serving a ten-year sentence for drug dealing.

Raised in Harlem Heights, a south Fort Myers neighborhood that had roots as a migrant farming community of mostly black and Hispanic residents, Eric Rivera Sr. grew up around drug dealers. He readily became one.

"I was raised by a single parent," said Rivera Sr., whose father, Luis Rivera, divorced his mother and moved to Boston when he was seven. "I had two brothers and one sister. I grew up playing sports. Drugs were out there. My mom, she worked two or three jobs to support us. That was the situation there."

Wilfred Rivera, Eric Sr.'s older brother, got into drug dealing first.

"We ended up making easy money," said Eric Rivera Sr., who would have graduated from Cypress Lake High School in 1988. Instead, he followed the lead of his older brother, just like he always did. "I got into it. I ended up dropping out of school and making the easy money."

The late 1980s marked a transitional period in the Fort Myers drug trade. Ronnie Tape and Larry White, the two biggest drug dealers from the early to mid-1980s, had been caught and incarcerated, leaving the door open for their successors.

"We were part of the next roundup," Rivera Sr. said. "We took over after they left. We were the biggest suppliers in this area when they went down."

Easy money led to hard time.

"Operation Catch-22," in which Lee County sheriff's deputies made twenty-two arrests in February 1990, had arrived. Deputies arrested Rivera Sr.'s mother as part of the operation. "That right there crushed me," Rivera Sr. said. The actions of the Rivera brothers implicated their mother because their business took place under the roof of her home. "Me getting locked up wasn't so bad, because I knew what I was doing was wrong," Rivera Sr. said. "I knew then that I'd never put my mom through that crap again."

"This is a big-time trend," Rivera Sr. said of Fort Myers children growing up with their fathers in prison. "I grew up in prison. I spent all of my twenties in prison. The main thing I learned is I never wanted to put myself in a position to separate myself from my family again. I saw a lot of things. I met a lot of kids my age who were never going to get out of prison. I was making easy money for a short amount of time. I was sixteen, seventeen, eighteen. It didn't take me long once I got to prison for me to realize that it wasn't worth it."

Rivera Sr.'s wife and children visited him almost every week. He passed most of his time playing sports: football, basketball, and softball. He read a lot of books. He earned his GED and took vocational classes in woodworking and brick masonry.

When Rivera Sr. was released from prison, Rivera Jr. was ten and just beginning to love football. Rivera Sr. became his son's coach, passing a background check because his felony did not involve a crime against a minor and took place more than seven years prior to submitting his coaching application. Rivera Sr. joined the Fort Myers Firecats, the same organization for which Deion Sanders had played youth football when it was known as the Fort Myers Rebels.

"It wasn't a big transition for me when I got out," Rivera Sr. said, in part because he found a legitimate job, working for a hurricane shutter company. He made six hundred to one thousand dollars per week for two years before suffering a back injury and losing the job. He then became a delivery truck driver, contracting for Sears until starting his own delivery company. He named it J & E Trucking, after his daughter Jericka and Eric Jr.

Rivera Sr. acknowledged the uncommonness of staying married to Annisha while being incarcerated for ten years. Annisha, her maiden name Churchwell, grew up in Dunbar, and her own immediate family often faced trouble with the law. Annisha's father dealt heroin. Her mother was arrested for allegedly shooting a gun at a school. Her brother twice was convicted of attempted murder. Another brother stood trial for manslaughter. Annisha avoided arrests, Rivera Sr. said, although law enforcement often followed her, deeming her guilty by association. She had lawful employment as a nurse and avoided the path taken by her father and brothers.

Alphonso Churchwell Sr., Rivera Jr.'s grandfather, went by a number of street names. Some called him "Jumpy." Others called him "Milkman" because he delivered heroin daily. Others called him the "King of the Hill."

"He was a tall guy, pretty strong, and he was truly bad," retired Lee County Sheriff's Capt. Kerry Griner told the *News-Press*. He worked narcotics in the 1980s. Churchwell sold "boy" and "girl" heroin. The former would be wrapped in aluminum foil shiny side out. The latter was sold shiny side in.

"He was a notorious badass and a drug dealer," Griner said. "A lot of people in the drug world think they're bad. But he really was. And that was in the true days when physical fighting made you a tough guy. Now it seems like people just settle it all with guns."

In 1982, the cops caught on to Alphonso Churchwell Sr.'s heroin trade. At age thirty-one, he was arrested for trafficking $2,500 worth of heroin off Anderson Avenue. Given a twenty-five-year sentence, he served only five years before running back to the street life again. Moving in and out of prison became Churchwell's modus operandi. He went back to prison after sheriff's deputies seized $44,000 worth of crack cocaine in "Operation Crackdown" in the mid-1980s. Released again, he went back to prison in 1989 on a grand theft auto charge.

"Her parents were in prison for most of her childhood," Rivera Sr. said of his wife. "She was put in a situation where she had to grow up at a young age."

While Annisha grew up to become a registered nurse, her brothers, Eric Rivera Jr.'s uncles, grew up to be like their father.

High-speed car chases, cocaine possession, cocaine trafficking, violent crimes, you name it, and two of Alphonso Churchwell Sr.'s sons were implicated in it. Alfonso Churchwell Jr. and Alvis Churchwell each received eight- to ten-year sentences for a variety of crimes while in their twenties.

Eric Rivera Sr. and Annisha did their best to shield Rivera Jr. from the dark side of the Churchwell family. Almost six years passed following Taylor's murder and Rivera Jr.'s arrest, and the trial had been postponed ten times. Finally, on November 4, 2013, a Miami Dade County jury convicted Rivera Jr. of second-degree murder. Three of his alleged accomplices were still awaiting trial.

On January 23, 2014, Rivera Jr. received a 57½-year prison sentence.

Rivera Sr. learned of Taylor's murder while watching his favorite TV show, ESPN's *Sports Center*.

"It wouldn't even have crossed my mind," Rivera Sr. said, that his son would end up being arrested, charged, and convicted of the crime. "The only time he'd go to Miami was when he was with us. My son was the quietest kid you could run into."

On the day of his son's arrest, Rivera Sr. received a phone call. The news stunned him. Looking back, he said a turning point happened in his son's life when he dropped out of Dunbar High School and ended up at Florida Christian Institute, which fielded a football team that included players who had dropped out of other, more traditional high schools.

"He had friends over there," Rivera Sr. said. "But he ended up either skipping school or going to school late all the time. That was our biggest mistake, letting him to go that school. It was a place where the kids went to school, and the kids ended up doing whatever they wanted to."

I could not reach Rivera Jr. to comment for this book for two reasons. First, he was under a gag order from his lawyers and then later from the judge leading up to his trial and subsequent conviction. Second, he was being transported from Dade County to prison at press time. I did, in March 2014, reach out to his father one more time for closure.

Eric Rivera Sr. said he believed his son's courtroom testimony that he actually was not the triggerman in Taylor's murder and that he was in the car, waiting outside when it happened. Rivera Sr. also, however, acknowledged that his son made the poorest of decisions in making that trip across the state that November night in 2007.

"What is it going to take for some of these kids to realize that this is not the route to go?" Rivera Sr. said. "I use my son as an example all the time when I talk to kids when I'm coaching football. He made a bad decision that got him to the point he's at now."

Edwina Churchwell, Eric Jr.'s grandmother, had kind words for her grandson.

"He was such a mannerable child," she told the *News-Press*, shortly after his arrest. "Anything you ask him to do, it was always, 'Yes, sir, yes, ma'am.' He was always a little gentleman. He had good parents. I just think he was falling into the wrong crowd."

Edwina Churchwell also once ran with the wrong crowd. In her mid-fifties, she managed a thrift store off Martin Luther King Jr. Blvd. But in 1986, while in her mid-thirties, she was arrested for trespassing following an argument with a friend that had spilled into the courtyard of Franklin Park Elementary school. Edwina Churchwell and her friend were wrestling over her gun when it fired, injuring no one. The incident took place across the street from Handy, Bassie, Armstrong, and Ellington Courts, across the street from the Dunbar strip of streets known as Left Corner.

Leaving Left Corner

A murder on Left Corner happened just before 1:30 a.m. Saturday, November 18, 1978, on Armstrong Court, the street named for jazz great Louis Armstrong. It happened outside the home of a woman named Dixie Blue, the girlfriend of Larry "Broadway Joe" Davenport.

Hit men believed to be from Sarasota and Miami shot Davenport seven times—four times in the chest, once in the stomach, and twice in the legs, according to the police report, which described the murder as drug-related. Davenport had encroached upon a rival drug dealer's territory. Davenport, nicknamed after New York Jets quarterback Joe Namath because Davenport had played quarterback with a similar style and flair, died at the scene. He was twenty-two.

Just as Jevon Kearse's father was murdered before Jevon Kearse was born, Larry Davenport was murdered before Najeh Davenport was born.

Najeh Davenport went by his mother's maiden name of Howard while growing up in Dunbar. He played running back at the University of Miami and then for seven seasons in the NFL, including 2002–5 with the Green Bay Packers.

"My father had three kids, all around the same time," said Najeh Davenport, who played Little League baseball with Earnest Graham and against Phillip Buchanon. Davenport moved to Miami after the sixth grade, graduating from Miami Central High.

"My brother and I became close," Najeh Davenport said. "We started hearing the stories about our father and how he died. I was like nine. I went to the Fort Myers library. They had these microfilm machines. I just remember going back to November 1978. I just read everything that I could that was reported on him.

"My mom and I left Fort Myers when I was twelve. Every time I came back, somebody was locked up, or somebody had died. So I stopped coming back."

Upon moving to Miami, Davenport chose to drop his mother's maiden name and take on the name of the father he never knew. Davenport later visited Fort Myers several times a year; his mother moved back, taking a job at Riverdale High.

"I chose to honor him," Davenport said of his name change. "In Fort Myers, everybody knew everybody. It's a small town. To this day, Fort Myers is OK, but I'm there for forty-eight hours and then I get out and then I'm gone."

Living in Fort Myers as a youth athlete shaped Najeh Davenport into the professional football player he became. He recalled racing down the hallway of his apartment complex against an older, Hispanic kid.

"We raced every day," Davenport said. "Sometimes, five, six times a day. Racing, racing, racing. We were on the third floor back then. I could never beat him. And then the day I beat him, I never wanted to race him again after that. Fort Myers, I believe it was just a different type of competition."

Competitions sometimes didn't end well in Fort Myers.

Another murder on Left Corner happened just before 1:30 a.m. on Friday, January 27, 2012. It happened on Ellington Court, named for jazz great Duke Ellington. It happened at the home of Altemia Diggs, a woman who graduated from Cypress Lake High School in 1985. She has been at the center of Dunbar's triumphs and tragedies, from generations both behind and ahead of her.

Constantine Bailey, better known as "Mr. B" and as a handyman who helped renovate Altemia Diggs's home, died that night from a gunshot wound to the chest. The first of a record twenty-four murders in Fort Myers in 2012 remained unsolved. A man, believed by the police to be driving a gray Toyota Scion, knocked on the door and shot Mr. B when he opened it, before fleeing.

Bailey and Altemia Diggs were engaged. Shed Diggs, Altemia's first husband, was in prison for drug dealing. They were divorced.

"I never stopped loving him," Altemia said of Shed Diggs. "I just decided to move on."

Mr. B grew up in Jamaica and worked for a power company. When he and Altemia Diggs began dating, she kept their relationship hidden from her children.

"Just let me be a friend to them," Mr. B insisted. "You're going to risk losing them to the streets while they're waiting for their dad? I don't have to be their dad. I can just be a friend to them."

That January night, Altemia Diggs lost her future husband, and her children lost their friend.

Altemia Diggs and her life story encompassed much that has happened in Dunbar. Her uncle, James Stephens, received one of those first three college football scholarships out of Dunbar High in 1949. She dated Deion Sanders. Her ex-husband, Shed, played football at Cypress Lake High School and the University of South Carolina as a linebacker. He began using and dealing drugs after knee injuries ended his NFL aspirations. Her oldest son, Jeremy Ware, played eight NFL games at cornerback for the Oakland Raiders as a seventh-round draft pick out of Michigan State in 2010.

"I honestly don't remember where I was when he got drafted," said Altemia Diggs, who wants her community to stress academics over football. "But I do know where I was when he graduated from college."

Her son Justin Diggs spent several months in prison for dealing drugs.

Her son Jordan Diggs ascended to high school football All-American status at Bishop Verot and Island Coast High Schools as a safety before following his father's football legacy at South Carolina, the same college that produced Dunbar's first NFL player in Johnnie Wright.

Altemia Diggs had weathered quite a few storms in her Ellington

Court home, but a fear unlike any other entered her heart that violent January night.

Devoted to her troubled neighborhood, Altemia renovated her mother's home after a fire, expanding it with the help of Mr. B into the largest and nicest home in Left Corner. Mr. B's murder made her rethink staying there.

"I never thought I would want to leave my home," Altemia said, six months after the murder. It took her more than two months to return to living there, having spent the interim living with a friend. "It's just getting so crazy. It just always seemed like somebody should be doing something for the neighborhood. I just felt like my little segment of the Diggs family would be that example. But right now, it's getting bad."

Left Corner wasn't always synonymous with drug dealing, Altemia said. Prior to the late 1970s, she said, it was the upper-class black neighborhood in Dunbar.

"Principals, teachers, nurses," she said. "People like that lived in that neighborhood. That was the atmosphere of the neighborhood at that time. We were more like the kids who were expected to do well. My grandmother and grandfather had been married for forty years. My father and mother separated. My mother was a live-in nanny."

Altemia Diggs's mother worked for Thomas DiBenedetto, a white Fort Myers resident who owned a minority stake in the Boston Red Sox.

"We were allowed to dream," Altemia said. "Those families were very good to us coming up. We were able to see a different lifestyle. I never bought into the ghetto mentality. The weekends, my mom would take us out there to go and help her clean. For me, people say, why would I want a house so big? I'd be eight years old, thinking, 'Someday, I'm going to have a house like this.' I knew that there was more than what was around here or what was being offered.

"I tried to do the same thing when I raised my kids. I raised my kids telling them that there was more for them. My grandfather owned a nightclub, and my grandmother owned a beauty salon. Growing up in that environment, people were making their own money. Now, I struggle. It doesn't come easy. I work so many hours. They don't understand that bills have to be paid."

Altemia Diggs owned and operated a beauty salon in Fort Myers and sold bail bonds on the side. She opened a salon off Anderson Avenue in Fort Myers in 1986. She was twenty-one, and her son Jeremy Ware was born on September 18 of that year. She went on to raise three more sons, a stepson, and two daughters. Daughter Jireh's birth nearly coincided with the accidental burning of their home. At that point, the rebuilding and the renewal began.

Shed Diggs spent 1993–98 in prison. He was convicted of drug dealing again after getting released, going back to prison in 2008.

"It just threw me," Altemia said. "I didn't even realize he was using again. He was coaching Pop Warner football. He was just doing so well. I really felt bad for him, because in all honesty, he was not dealing drugs. But because he shared them, it was considered distributing."

Shed Diggs had earned a master's degree in biblical studies and a bachelor's in criminal justice with a minor in juvenile delinquency at South Carolina. After already having served five years in prison, he received a ten-year sentence upon the second offense.

Left Corner no longer resembled the neighborhood of Altemia's childhood. Altemia forbid her children to walk just one block over to Bassie Court because of the drugs being sold there.

"We don't get to come home and see moms and dads who get to be doctors or lawyers," Jordan Diggs said, just before leaving for South Carolina for his freshman year in 2012. "We don't have the big houses. We play football in the streets from the time the sun comes up to when the sun comes down. That's how we do it. You play football. Coming up, sports are what keep you out of the streets. Going to practice, hustling in school in order to play sports, that's what motivates us. For me, if I brought home a 'C,' I knew I was going to get it.

"Playing sports is what keeps us out of the streets. When you're surrounded by that stuff, sports don't always save every kid. Nowadays, it's not like how it was back in the day. You don't have guys [drug dealers] handing kids money to keep them off the streets. You don't have guys giving them money to go buy shoes. Times are too hard. It's a totally different ballgame."

Even before his teenage years, Jordan Diggs aspired to be like his father, Shed—not by selling drugs but by excelling at football—and doing so at South Carolina.

"My dad played all four years of college at South Carolina. Tore his ACL. Played with the Vikings and got cut," Jordan Diggs said. "He tore one knee, came back and tore another one. He played in the Canadian league for a little bit. He missed home. The Canadian league wasn't very deep. In my eyes, my dad is one of the greatest football players ever. That's just how I view him. If he hadn't gotten hurt, there's no doubt he would have been an NFL player."

Sitting in his mother's beauty salon, Jordan Diggs recognized the beauty of his situation.

"I want to be an NFL superstar," Jordan Diggs said. "I started playing at five. I skipped a level." He then named some players who had achieved greatness at the high school level and advanced to Division I football.

"Jaylen Watkins, Desmond Kearse, Schon Thomas. I played with those guys," Jordan Diggs said. "Once I found out I could compete with them, my dream really began there. My whole family being football-oriented, there wasn't even a choice. I wanted to give it my all."

Jordan Diggs gave it his all at Bishop Verot High. Like Mario Henderson before him, Jordan Diggs said he had trouble fitting in with the academic and social scene at a predominantly white school.

"I wasn't comfortable there," Jordan Diggs said. "These are the kids that live on McGregor Boulevard. These are the kids who live in Fiddlesticks. It's just two different cultures. From the first day in school, I was 'the black kid.' Put yourself in my shoes. It wasn't a comfortable setting for me. It did give me a foundation, an academic structure. But when I went to Island Coast, I hadn't even been there a whole week when I took a test. And boom, I passed it just like that.

"I could tell you a million stories about what I went through at Verot. It's one of those things that made me the person I am now. At Verot, it's cool to be smart. In a public school setting, if you're a kid answering all the questions in class, then you're the geek. You're the nerd. At Verot, you have kids whose lives are already planned out.

"When I got to Island Coast, I started realizing how good I was in football. It was a confidence builder for me. It was a learning experience."

Should Jordan Diggs reach the NFL, he said, he would leave Fort Myers and Dunbar behind him.

"I love my city," Jordan Diggs said. "I would always come back and visit. But this is not where I want to make my home. This is not where I want to raise my kids. Even though I'm thankful for having to face my struggles, this is not where I want to be. There's nothing like being here. There's nothing like growing up here.

"Deion Sanders, Anthony Henry, Phillip Buchanon, Jevon Kearse, they could all be here right now. But they're not. They're all gone. Other people have their struggles. If you go through what you go through here, that just gives you your hunger. Our life is a constant struggle."

When the topic turned to the murder of Mr. B, Jordan Diggs had trouble talking about it. Jordan Diggs was on the verge of leaving his home for good.

"I was raised there," Jordan Diggs said of the house in which Mr. B lost his life. "Born and raised. That was just crazy. It just tells you how crazy this area is getting. I've got eight more days and counting."

Shed Diggs rooted for all of his children to succeed. While in prison, he wrote me a letter dated October 24, 2010. "I have made some bad choices in my life up until this point," Shed Diggs wrote. "I have hurt a lot of people who loved me unconditionally. Because of the bad choices I have made in life, I have caused them a lot of heartaches, sleepless nights, and hard times with the economy the way it is.

"I have made some bad choices when it came to my marriage, too. I may not have nothing when I get home, no wife, no car, no home or anything. But I'm standing on the promise of a man, and that man is Jesus, because right now, all I have is Him. I see it like this. All of this humiliation and the trials I'm going through just gives Christ an opportunity to demonstrate his power through me when I'm released."

Diggs quoted 2 Corinthians 5, verse 17: "If any man be in Christ, he is a new creature; old things are passed away, behold all things have become new."

"So that's me," Shed Diggs wrote. "A reconditioned man."

Not far from Left Corner, in the Harlem Lakes neighborhood, grew up high school All-American wide receiver Sammy Watkins IV.

In 1977, Sammy Watkins Sr., the great-grandfather of Watkins IV and the father of eleven children, was delivering bundles of the *News-Press* to newsstands and convenience stores. An unknown assassin gunned him down just south of Anderson Avenue.

In 2010, Sammy Watkins IV made his mark on Lee County high school football. He scored two touchdowns for South Fort Myers High in the final three minutes of a regional championship state playoff game against Bradenton Southeast. That propelled the Wolfpack to victory and cemented Watkins's status as a Lee County legend of high school football. Lee County's all-time leading high school wide receiver and an All-American at South Fort Myers High School signed with Clemson University. He vowed to steer clear of the drugs that could be seen dealt and the gunshots that could be heard fired from the picnic table outside his home.

Sammy Watkins IV's stepfather, James McMiller, raised Watkins from toddlerhood.

"It's like that old BASF commercial," said Donald Williams, a family friend. "He didn't make the product. He just made the product better."

Like Shed Diggs, McMiller had a history of selling drugs, in his case marijuana. Unlike Diggs, McMiller never got caught, never spending time in jail or prison.

Sammy Watkins IV and Jordan Diggs sprang from similar environments.

"If you have two parents in the household, you have a better chance of being successful and achieving the goals you want," McMiller said. "But if you have parents who are so consumed with work, then you might as well have no parents. In Dunbar, they're living in poverty. Their job is food, clothes, and roof over your head. They're so consumed with that, that they don't have time to smell the roses. Sniff. It's a beautiful day. I have a great wife. I have a *great* wife. These are the things that motivated me to keep going to work. For me, my kids saved my life.

"In a nutshell, the ghetto is looked upon and frowned upon as a very bad place. In reality, there's a lot of love here. We all stick together."

McMiller began selling drugs during his junior and senior years at Cypress Lake High School in 1988–89. He weighed on the south side of 100 pounds and at five foot six had no football future. He aspired to be a boxer. Maybe he could have been the next Pernell Whitaker or Floyd Mayweather Jr. McMiller's father, however, never showed up to his son's fights, even after McMiller went to the Junior Olympics and won the Sunshine State games in 1988.

"My dad was one of those workaholics," McMiller said. "I wanted him to be very, very proud of me, which he was. But I could never get him to a boxing match. So I felt deprived when I was young. By me not having that, I ended up quitting boxing.

"I ended up going to the street, trying to move product. During that time, I ran into all kinds of obstacles. I ran into guys who robbed and had trouble with the law. Relationship-wise, it's a strain. If you have a good girl who's steady, it puts a strain on you. I hung out and watched my friends make money. They had money, and I had nothing."

In 1992, McMiller said he simply quit the drug dealing.

"My main thing is coming home and having my kids proud of me," said McMiller, who maintained his job as a truck driver, even as his stepson Sammy Watkins enrolled at Clemson. "It's not the best job in the world, but it's not the worst job in the world.

"You take life lessons. You learn from your mistakes. There's nothing out there that could get me out there selling drugs now. Because I know that there are always alternatives rather than to go out there and get myself in trouble. Who knows? Sammy might not be where he is had I not quit. What you do, in your job as a parent, is you never give up on your kids. You don't stop being a parent until you die. At forty-two years old, I can learn like a baby. You never stop learning. You want to keep a broad mind. Your spectrum has to be wide.

"I want to be wealthy, but if that's not in the cards for me, that's God's plan. Faith is very, very big in the black community. Thank you, Jesus. Thank you, Lord."

From prison, Shed Diggs said for all of its uniqueness, there are other neighborhoods with the same dark temptations as Dunbar. He would continue to pray for those men and women and their children.

"Anywhere you go in the world, you're gonna have a neighborhood like Left Corner," Shed Diggs wrote from prison. "But again, it's about the choices you make. For me, I know now that what looks good is not always good for you. As a kid in the Left Corner, my internal tape recorder was running at all times, so I saw a lot of the drug game being put down, but for a while none of the guys would want me around.

"They would hurry and give me money for me to stay in school, and to stay on that football field, and this was like that for me all the way through college. Somewhere after graduating from the University of South Carolina, I lost focus on life and started messing around with drugs, and it seems like that old devil or slave master never stopped riding me.

"I believe football is one way out of the 'hood, but kids need to broaden their horizons and reach for the sky, because there are so many opportunities out there.

"We, the people of Dunbar, as a community need unity first no matter what the cause. We need to embrace every kid with love and help them achieve their aspirations in life. Somewhere I lost my fire and passion and started back doing drugs and dabbling again. If I could take it all back and do it again, I would. But I can't, so I made this bed, and I'm going to deal with it when I get out."

. . . .

The cycle continues in Dunbar and in Fort Myers.

On May 8, 2014, Sammy Watkins became the No. 4 pick in the NFL Draft. The Buffalo Bills selected him following his record-setting career at Clemson University and his Most Valuable Player performance in the Orange Bowl. Sammy Watkins signed a four-year rookie contract worth $19.9 million, including a $12.8 million signing bonus. Two days later, the Philadelphia Eagles made Jaylen Watkins, Sammy's half-brother, the first pick of the fourth round and the 101st overall selection. Meanwhile, Sammy Watkins's half-brother Jari McMiller was serving a 20-month prison sentence for a felony weapons charge.

Jordan Diggs prepared for his sophomore season at South Carolina, hoping to climb his way onto a future NFL Draft board.

Retired Tampa Bay Buccaneer Earnest Graham bought a house in 2013 in Cape Coral, where he played high school football at Mariner, just a few miles from Dunbar. He set up an insurance business in Fort Myers, within walking distance of the streets known as The Bottom, where his mother grew up and not far from where his grandfather once made and sold shoes.

Graham also entered 2014 in his first year as high school football coach, helming the program—North Fort Myers High School—that produced future NFL players Deion Sanders, Jevon Kearse, Richard Fain, and Warren Williams, all former Dunbar residents. Graham said he intended to use his platform as a high school coach as a form of ministry through football, trying to stop the cycle of drugs and violence in his hometown.

While Ronnie Tape awaited his fall 2014 release from a halfway house after spending more than twenty-five years in prison, his grandson Ronnie Tape III was attending college. Tape III started at quarterback as a senior in 2012 for the Gateway Charter High football team in Fort Myers, graduating in May 2013.

While Deion Sanders maintained his Hall of Fame presence as an NFL Network analyst and continued to work with the low-income children of Dallas, the Fort Myers High School football team mourned the shooting death of sophomore running back JoJo Brunson, caught in the crossfire of a gang turf war in April 2013 in Dunbar. A year later, the murder remained unsolved.

While Alto Henry, Joe Kearse Jr., and Brandon Graham lived month to month, finding work where they could in Naples, Fort Myers, and Tampa, their brothers Anthony Henry, Jevon Kearse, and Earnest Graham continued to live lives of luxury, having earned millions as NFL players.

While Shed Diggs awaited his own release from prison, his son Jordan Diggs awaited what he hoped to be a stellar sophomore season at South Carolina, the school at which some of the seeds of Dunbar's NFL aspirations were planted, where Johnnie Wright became the first man from Dunbar to play in the NFL in 1983.

These neighborhood legends all were interconnected. More were on the way. More would have to navigate the triumphs and the tragedies of Dunbar, where children always seemed to be facing fourth down, scrambling and hoping for a way to finish first.

Acknowledgments

I'm certain that this book, my first, would not have been possible without the people from the neighborhoods in the area known as Dunbar. So many current and former NFL players shared their stories with the hope of bettering their community. Jammi German and Levon Simms gave me valuable insight. All of the NFL players mentioned in this book—and in many cases their parents and grandparents—were instrumental in making this happen.

Life in Fort Myers never would have happened for me had my friend Ben Grove not shown me a flyer in 1994 within the walls of the William Allen White School of Journalism at the University of Kansas. My three-month internship at the *News-Press* evolved into a lifelong career. KU journalism professors Tom Eblen and Susanne Shaw prepared me for this journey. Sam Sul and Anh Sul, Roger Hartwick, Chris English, Dave Platt, and all of my other Jayhawk friends supported this.

Others who played a big role were my teachers at the Choate Rosemary Hall boarding school. Doug James, Chip Lowery, and Charlie Long sharpened my work ethic. Friends Andrew Sell, Stefan Baytarian, and everyone else at Jessup Red, East Cottage, and Memorial Gardens influenced me.

Very special thanks go to Ronnie Tape for sharing details of his story and for telling the up-and-coming Dunbar children and teenagers what not to do. He did the crime, but he served his time. When the time is right, I hope Tape will come back to Fort Myers and make a positive impact on his hometown. Rosemary Tape, Douglas Frazier, and Rochelle Reback also were instrumental with the Tape chapter.

Everyone at the *News-Press* and news-press.com assisted me in one way or another. I'm going to thank many of them here by name. My thanks to every past and current member of the sports department, especially Mike Klocke, the sports editor who hired me, and Sam Cook, who took a keen interest in developing my reporting and writing skills. Tom Hayden, Virginia Lewis, and especially Mark Bickel and Ed Reed assigned me stories, as well as the Tampa Bay Buccaneers beat in 2006–8, which helped create this book. Current staff writers Dan Deluca, Craig Handel, and Seth Soffian have been especially supportive. Other current and former *News-Press* staffers who helped or inspired include: Jim Greenhill, Bob Norman, and Brittany Norman; Pat Gillespie, Rachel Myers, and Janine Zeitlin; photographers J. D. Emmett, Kinfay Moroti, Marc Beaudin, Molly Beaudin, Sarah Coward, Garth Francis, Jack Hardman, Amanda Inscore, Ben Rusnak, Lindsay Terry, Guy Tubbs, K. T. Warnke, Andrew West, Terry Allen Williams, and Ricardo Rolon; Scott Noll and Irv Harrell; Roger Williams, Melanie Payne, Lee Melsek, and Peter Franceschina; Steve Bacon, Scott Bihr, Carl Bleich, Terry Brady, Betsy Clayton, Francesca Donlan, Tim Engstrom, Joe Fenton, Wendy Fullerton, Robyn George, Keith Gibson, Aaron Greenfield, Dayna Harpster, John Harris, Denes Husty, Mary Ann Husty, Andrew Jarosh, David Kaye, Ron Kaspriske, Bill Kilpatrick, Tariq Lee, Doug MacGregor, Cindy McCurry-Ross, Glenn Miller, David Moulton, Barry Obenchain, Cory O'Donnell, Paula Parrish, David Plazas, Mike Purdy, Ronnie Ramos, Bob Rathgeber, Charles Runnells, Gary Sharp, Pete Sisk, Gabriella Sousa, Deron Snyder, Byron Stout, Chris Umpierre, Chris Walsh, Rick Weber, and Sheldon Zoldan. Executive editor Terry Eberle, Kate Marymont, publishers Mei-Mei Chan and Carol Hudler, and every other newspaper writer and editor I have known over the years have been valuable friends and influences.

Many mistakes in the earlier drafts were caught by Brad Windsor. Mark Stephens helped me trim some of the fat near the end and emerged at the right time as an invaluable first reader and resource. Mike Donlan did a fantastic job with the map. Literary agents Scott

Waxman and David Larabell helped me refocus the narrative. Randy Wayne White urged me to be relentless. Joe Drape, a fellow Kansan and author of *Our Boys*, provided a vital critique, prompting me to add a personal touch in the final stages.

You can't write without the support of fellow writers. They include: Steve Rushin, Buster Olney, Tom Verducci, Michael McKnight, Darcy Frey, Jeff Pearlman, Stefan Fatsis, Michael Kruse, Jay Jennings, Travis Waters, Trent Toone, Robert Andrew Powell, Gordon Edes, Dan Shaughnessy, Scott Miller, LaVelle Neal III, Joe Christensen, Mike Berardino, Dave Campbell, Roy Cummings, Ira Kaufman, Stephen Holder, Rick Stroud, Will Graves, Tony Masarotti, Richard Deitsch, Nathan Whitaker, Peter King, and Joe Satriani. From Fort Myers, I also would like to thank Barry Hendon, Marcus Sherry, Mike Corso, Brandon Rose, Wally Bixby, and Jim Doepke. I thank Terry Ryan, Bill Smith, and Ron Gardenhire of the Minnesota Twins, and anyone else who has made me smile at Fort Myers Miracle games and Twins and Boston Red Sox spring-training games.

"Wilkiemania" architect Donnie Wilkie must be mentioned for his support along with Bill Pollock, Ron Riley, Chris Diller, John Cavell, Donny Overholser, and of course Dick Vitale and the rest of the City of Palms Classic clan. Neal and Janna Trottier, Mike Hulse, Mary Hulse, and Mike McQuagge deserve mention, as do Sam Henderson of Moore Haven fame, Will Prather, Al Hanser, LeDondrick Rowe, John Carrigan, Dr. Bo Kagan, Dr. John Kagan, Judge John Carlin, Tad Yeatter, and Fort Myers mayor Randy Henderson. The entire Lee County football community, especially the coaches, athletic directors, principals, Margaret Sirianni, Dave La Rosa, Superintendent Nancy Graham, and former superintendent James Browder deserve praise for their efforts with these children, as do Bill Kramer and John Weber. Robert Steele, Dominic Jemella, Dave Capel, Sam Sirianni Sr., Wade Hummel, Mike Hoyem, Steve Bumm, Rosella Wright, Brenda Kearse, and Sandra Smith died before the completion of this book, as did my grandparents. They are missed.

If not for the University Press of Florida, I would not have had the opportunity to share this book with so many readers. Thank you to

Shannon McCarthy, Susan Murray, Rachel Doll, Teal Amthor-Shaffer, Larry Leshan, Marthe Walters, and the rest of the staff and committee for believing in *Fourth Down in Dunbar*.

First Christian Church of Fort Myers deserves thanks, as do Pastor Gary Cox and Linda Cox, John Meredith and Donna Meredith, Tina Church and Rodger Church, Evelyn Strader, and all of my Kenyan companions, Joey Potter, Dexter Davis, and Brian Lynch.

Emily Stone and Samuel Dorsey, my children, each provided an equal amount of inspiration. My mother-in-law, Vicki; John and Dahlia Wright; and grandmother MommoBobbie also deserve credit for encouragement.

Gene and Nancy Dorsey, my parents, taught and inspired me to read and write. I could not have done this without them. My brothers, Mark, Todd, and Kyle, are awesome. I am blessed to have such good parents and brothers, sister-in-law Gina, and new nephew Jackson.

Bonnie Kayleen Stone Dorsey, my wife, the one who knows and finally led me to Jesus, who encouraged me to finish this project, and has been here for me in ways she cannot even imagine, is also my best friend. She was the Riverdale High prom queen, and her grace and beauty increase with each passing day. I love you. Thank you for sticking with this. She's by far the Greatest of All Time from Fort Myers.

Note on Sources

Although the reporting for *Fourth Down in Dunbar* began upon my arrival in Fort Myers, Florida, in 1994, I did not realize that until 2008, when I decided to write this book.

From 2008 through the earliest weeks of 2014, I relied on my previous reporting in the *News-Press* in developing the sources, and in several instances, using quotes gathered in Southwest Florida's oldest newspaper.

Most of the book consists of interviews conducted on my own time and apart from my duties at the *News-Press*. Many of those interviews and connections made, however, would have been impossible without the newspaper and my role there. At times, some of my newspaper story ideas flowed from the heart of this book, and vice versa.

I cite below a few articles of mine and a few by my colleagues from which I used quotes or information.

"A Tale of Two Grahams," from July 26, 2008, helped me form the Earnest Graham chapter. If not for the cooperation of Earnest and Brandon Graham and their late mother, Sandra Smith, this book may not have existed. I gathered quotes from former Tampa Bay Buccaneers linebacker Barrett Ruud and former coach Jon Gruden while working for the *News-Press*.

The "33916: Life on the Edge" project, reported and written by Janine Zeitlin and published June 13–15, 2010, became a remarkable resource for the statistics in chapter 4, "Dunbar's Dynamics." Zeitlin wrote the series in order to spotlight the higher crime, unemployment, high school dropout, teen pregnancy, and low-infant birth rates of the Dunbar neighborhoods, hoping to give community leaders the awareness that would help them to try to turn around these social ills.

Although I was the first reporter to interview Noel Devine at length, in the summer of 2005, Devine declined all further interview requests from me. I therefore relied on two stories I wrote: "Football Star Primed for New Life," from June 17, 2005, and "Devine Departure Big Mess," from July 29, 2005, for a large portion of chapter 16, "Noel Devine." The latter article was co-written with Deron Snyder. Colleague Dan Deluca's "The Long Run," from July 1, 2012, helped me finish the Devine chapter, as did the video interview produced by Kinfay Moroti.

"Dunbar High Graduates Blazed a Trail, Then Molded Lives," from August 29, 2010, laid the groundwork for chapter 2, on Safety Hill.

"Abrupt Ending: Injury Derailed Cypress Star's Career," which ran July 17, 2011, helped me get to know Don Ellis and begin constructing chapter 6, "Before Prime."

"Felonies Run in Suspect's Family," written by Rachel Myers and published December 16, 2007, assisted me in reporting chapter 17, on Sean Taylor, and the Associated Press helped me finish it with news of Eric Rivera Jr.'s sentencing.

Several News-Press stories from the 1970s, written by Lee Melsek, helped me piece together Jevon Kearse's family history. "Titans Defensive End Jevon Kearse Is Running in Circles," written by Michael Silver and published in Sports Illustrated on August 28, 2000, gave me a few important details about Kearse's history as well.

A cart full of courtroom transcripts provided research materials about Ronnie Tape, in addition to my interviews and e-mail exchanges with him.

Let's not forget Deion Sanders. His book Power, Money, & Sex: How Success Almost Ruined My Life was a valuable resource in getting to know Sanders better. The hours I spent with Helen Capel and the late Dave Capel discussing Sanders's youth were vital. Connie Knight, Deion's mother, provided valuable assistance here as well. This chapter would not have been possible without the News-Press paying for my two-day trip to North Dallas in January 2011, my trip to Super Bowl XLV on

February 6, 2011, and my trip to Canton, Ohio, in the summer of 2011 for Sanders's Pro Football Hall of Fame induction. I also gathered the quotes from Bobby Bowden about Sanders during my newspaper duties. The Pro Football Hall of Fame provided a transcript of Sanders's Hall of Fame speech.

I originally intended to include in this book other Southwest Florida NFL players who did not grow up in Dunbar neighborhoods. My interviews with these athletes were left on the cutting-room floor, but I would like to thank them for their time—and applaud them for their accomplishments: Spencer Adkins, Nate Allen, the late Sam Bailey, Tommy Bohanon, Jake O'Connell, Corey Lynch, Fred McCrary, Matt Prater, NFL official Jeff Rice, and recently retired NFL side judge Larry Rose. Edgerrin James especially went above and beyond with his time.

Between 2008 and 2014, while researching this book, I conducted personal interviews, apart from my duties at the *News-Press*, with the following, who are listed in order of appearance: Deion Sanders, Robert Green, Karl Morrison, Vera Stephens, Jeremiah Primus, Riley Ware, Frankie Raybon, Leon Church, Levon Simms, Larry Gary, Walt Wesley, Rosemary Tape, Johnnie Wright, Rosella Wright, Warren Williams Jr., George Rogers, Eric Riley, Don Ellis, Ronnie Tape, Gerald Copeland, Douglas Frazier, Walter Sutton, John Quintier, Shirley Chapman, Connie Knight, Dave Capel, Ron Hoover, Calvin Church, Johnie Church, Jammi German, Melvin German Sr., Sam Sirianni Jr., Jevon Kearse, Cisco Navas, Paul Kearse, Brenda Kearse, Essie Mae Robinson, Anthony Henry, Lee Peters, Joe Hampton, Anthony Dixon, Sammy Brown, Mike Sturgis, Jerrold Colton, Sandra Smith, Earnest Graham, Tim Maloney, Teddy Dupay, Mike Vogt, Michael McNerney, Alicia Graham, Lisa Martin, Steve Larsen, Earnest Graham Sr., Phillip Buchanon, James Buchanon, Mike Gill, Floridia Pickens, Mario Henderson, Jim Scarry, Mark Morehead, Scott Jones, Elizabeth Cody, Linnea Alexander, Terrence Cody, Jason Milliken, Maureen Milliken, Kourtney Kelly, Mark Carter, Johnny Carter, Eric Rivera Sr., Najeh Davenport, Altemia Diggs, Jordan Diggs, Shed Diggs, Jeremy Ware, Donald Williams, and James McMiller.

DAVID DORSEY writes and reports for the *Fort Myers (Fla.) News-Press* and has since 1994. He also has written for the *Kansas City Star* and *USA Today*. He grew up in Fairfield, Ohio; Plano and Kingwood, Texas; Yardley, Pennsylvania; and Yanbu, Saudi Arabia; he graduated from Choate Rosemary Hall in Wallingford, Connecticut, and the University of Kansas in Lawrence. He and his wife have a son, a grown daughter, three cats, and a crazy yellow lab named Thor.

Follow him on Twitter @DavidADorsey.